Cybersecurity

How to Protect Your Children and Family

Paul Felt

Contents

Introduction

Cybersecurity is the usage of protecting computers and servers, mobile devices, electronic systems, networks, and data from malicious attacks. Additionally, known as information technology security and electronic information security. The term applies to various environments, from business to mobile computing, and can be divided into several common categories.

- Network security is the practice of protecting computer networks from intruders (whether they are targeted attackers or opportunistic malware).
- Application security strives to protect software and devices from threats. The compromised application may provide access to data protected by its design. Successful security starts in the design phase before the deployment of the program or equipment.
- Information security can protect the integrity and privacy of data during storage and transmission.
- Operational security includes the processes and decisions used to process and protect data assets. The permissions that users have

when accessing the network and the process of determining how to store data and where to store or share data fall under this protection.

The Importance of Children's Cybersecurity

The Internet has developed into an easily accessible place, so it has also become essential to ensure security. Parents need to take the time to ensure the safety of their children on the Internet. If used properly, the Cyberworld can become a tool for information, learning, and connection. In addition to all these possibilities, there are potential injuries, but parents can make sure that their children learn to be safe if they are appropriately protected.

The continuous launch of new applications and social media sites allows children to be exposed to new things regularly. As a parent, your job is to provide your children with the right tools and knowledge to browse the web safely.

Teach Children About Internet Safety

The Internet is an ideal place for studying, shopping, playing games and talking with friends. Unluckily, there are also predators, identity thieves, and others who can harm you online. To be safe online, you and your children need to be aware of these dangers.

Several children are confident that they know how to stay online safely. However, some reasons usually put children at greater risk. They may not always consider the consequences of their actions, which may cause them to share too much information about themselves. Sometimes, cyberbullies or predators also explicitly target children.

If you are a parent or guardian, you can help ensure your children's safety by talking to your children about their Internet usage, teaching them about online dangers, and learning everything about the Internet to help ensure your children's safety and make informed decisions.

Understanding Online Dangers

To ensure the safety of your children, you need to understand the different types of online dangers that exist. For example, children and teenagers may find inappropriate content on the Internet, such as pornography or obscene language. It is also possible to be bullied or harassed by others online. This does not signify that your child will encounter all these threats. However, knowing the dangers can help you, or your children can also make informed decisions online.

Other Types of Danger

Whenever someone practices a computer, there is a danger of eye fatigue, wrist fatigue and other injuries. You can avoid this by checking the time your child spends on computers and mobile devices. For tips on preventing damage, read "Creating a Safe Work Area" in the "Computer Basics" tutorial.

Another reason for restricting children's use of the Internet is that as people spend more and more time on the Internet, Internet addiction has become a more severe problem. Internet use may be a good thing, but if addiction, it will affect a person's offline life.

A Place Where Danger May Occur

Kids need to be careful when connecting to the Internet because online dangers are not limited to harmful websites. Chat rooms, computer games, or even social networking sites can be risky. When your child has a mobile phone, you also need to be careful when sending text messages or accessing the Internet through a mobile phone.

Guidelines to Ensure the Safety of Children

Ensuring your child is completely safe online can be a challenge. Even when you set up parental controls on your home computer, your kids will use many other computers without parental controls. To ensure your children's safety, you need to teach them to make the right decisions online, even if you are not around.

Here are some general tips for teaching kids' online safety:

- Learn all about the Internet. Familiarity with the Internet can not only help you understand the risks but also help you talk to your children.
- Set standards for what your children can or cannot do online. It is essential to set rules for your children so they can know what is expected of them. Don't wait for terrible things to happen and start creating guidelines.
- Teach your children to keep personal information confidential. Publishing personal information (such as phone numbers, addresses, and credit cards) online is usually a bad idea. If criminals have access to this knowledge, they can use it to harm you and your family.
- Educate your kids to use social networking sites safely. Sites like Facebook allow children or adults to share photos and videos of themselves and have conversations with friends and strangers. If your child shares something with friends, it may still be mastered by the wrong person. Generally, they should publish content online only if they are satisfied with everyone in the world.
- If your child has a problem, encourage them to come to you. If your child is having trouble surfing the Internet, you will want him or her to come to you instead of hiding it. Keep in mind that even if they do everything right, your child may occasionally encounter a lousy website.
- Talk to your child about internet usage. Communicate to your children regularly about how they use the Internet. If they are used to discussing the Internet with you, they will be more willing to contact you when problems arise.

Children's Online Safety Rule

These rules are mainly for older minor children. The appropriate "rules" for online use vary with age, child maturity, and family values.

1. Without parental consent, I will not disclose personal information, such as my address, phone number, parent's work address/phone number.

2. When anything makes me feel uncomfortable, I will tell my parents immediately.

3. Without checking with my parents first, I would never agree to be with someone I "acquainted" online. When my parents agree to the meeting, I will ensure that the meeting is held in a public place and ask my parents to accompany it.

4. I will discuss with my parents about posting pictures of myself or others on the Internet, rather than assigning any opinions that my parents deem inappropriate.

5. I will not respond to any news that is mean or makes me feel uncomfortable in any way. I don't think it's my fault to get such a statement. When I do, I will tell my parents immediately.

6. I will talk to my parents so that we can make rules for surfing the Internet and using mobile phones. We will decide how long I can go online, how long I can go online, and the appropriate areas I can visit. Without their permission, I will not enter other sites or violate these rules.

7. I will not show the password to anyone other than my parents (even my best friend).

8. I will review with my parents before downloading and installing software or doing anything that may damage our computers or mobile devices or endanger the privacy of family members.

9. I will be an excellent online citizen or will not do anything to harm others or illegal.

10. I will help my parents know how to play and learn things online and teach them some knowledge about the Internet, computers and other technologies.

Cybersecurity Issues

The Internet may be a dangerous community for everyone, but children and young people are especially vulnerable. From online predators to social media posts, these posts may haunt them later, and cyber harm may bring serious, expensive, and even tragic consequences. Children may inadvertently expose their family members to Internet threats, such as accidentally downloading malware, which may allow cybercriminals to access their parents' bank accounts or other sensitive information. Defending children on the Internet is a matter of awareness-understanding the potential dangers and how to prevent them. Although network security software can help defend against specific threats, the primary security measure is open communication with children.

Cyberbullying

The vast majority (90%) of teenagers agree that cyberbullying is a problem, and 63% think it is a severe problem. A 2018 study of children's online behavior found that about 60% of children who use social media witnessed some form of bullying. For various reasons, most children completely ignore this behavior. As of February 2018, almost half (47%) of young people are victims of cyberbullying. Social media or online games are today's virtual playgrounds, where many cyberbullying behaviors have occurred and are running 24/7. Children can be smiled at in social media communications. In online games, their player characters may be attacked continuously, which turns the game from an imaginary adventure into an insulting test and gradually escalates to cyberbullying across multiple platforms and in real life.

The best basis for preventing cyberbullying is to talk to your child about what is happening online and in real life (IRL) and how to endure bullying. Internet security software and dedicated apps for monitoring children's online and mobile activities can help, but there is nothing to replace open conversations.

Cyber Predator

Today, sexual predators and other predators often use their innocence, lack of adult supervision, and abuse of trust to stalk children on the Internet. This may eventually lead to children being lured into dangerous individuals to encounter IRL. These predators lurk on social media or gaming platforms that attract children and virtual places where anonymous users participate in cyberbullying. Here, they can use not only the innocence of children but also their imagination. "Let's pretend" is a standard and healthy part of online games and interactive activities, but predators can use it as a hook to attract children. But, again, the best protection measure is to regularly talk to your children about what is happening in their daily lives.

Posting Private Information

The children have not still understood social boundaries. Both may post personally identifiable information (PII) online; for example, this information should not be published publicly in their social media profiles. From pictures of awkward personal moments to their home address or family vacation plans, this might be.

Most (but not all) of the information your child publishes is public. This means that you can see it too, and remind them that if mom and dad can see it, everyone else can view it. There is no harm. Avoid monitoring, but talk frankly with your child about public boundaries and what they mean for your child and the whole family.

Phishing

Cybersecurity experts call phishing the use of emails that try to trick people into clicking malicious links or attachments. It is challenging for children to detect these emails because it usually appears to be from a legitimate person, such as a friend or family member, just saying: "Hey, you might like this!" You can also use messaging apps or SMS to complete this operation and then called it "spoofing."

Phishing emails and dirty texts can pop up at any time. Still, cybercriminals who design such emails pay close attention to popular websites with children and collect information such as email addresses or friends' names, and other information to tailor Customize their attacks and the actions of spear-phishing websites when they access the company's network. Educate your children to avoid clicking on emails or texts from strangers, or be wary of messages that seem to be from their friends but appear to be "not at home" or have no real personal information.

Fall into A Scam

Children may not be obsessed with the Nigerian prince who offered them a million dollars, but they may fall for scams that provide cherished things, such as free use of online games or special features. Young people quickly become a sign of scams because they have not learned to be vigilant. Like phishing, cybercriminals can use websites popular with children to identify potential victims and then promise to provide rewards in exchange for what they want, such as parents' credit card information.

Whether you are old or old, the best way to prevent fraud is to know that it may not be correct if an offer sounds too good to be true. Teach your children not to be skeptical of online services that promise too much.

The Accidental Download of Malware

Malicious software is computer software installed without the victim's knowledge or permission and can perform harmful operations on the computer. This involves stealing personal information from your computer and hijacking that information for use in a "botnet", causing performance degradation. Cybercriminals often trick people into downloading malicious software. Phishing is one of these techniques, but other methods (for example, persuading victims to download malware disguised as games) can trick children.

As with scams, educating children is the best protection, but comprehensive cross-device network security software and related security protections can help protect children's computers from malware that sneaks into it. Many Internet safety products also include specific parental controls and applications that can help you establish a safe framework for your children's online activities.

Back to Posts That Bothered Children in Life

There is no "delete" button on the Internet. It is the opposite of Las Vegas. What happens, stay online. Forever and always. Anything your child puts online is almost impossible to delete later. The dangers of social media are daunting. Especially for teenagers, it is challenging to consider how gathering pictures or Snap-chat messages with in ten years of a new job interview can cause problems, or how prospective partners respond to their unique content media profiles or other websites posted on social networks.

Explain to your teenagers that their styles and opinions will change with age. They don't have a 15-year-old self; they need to click on it without having to click on the "retrieve" or "delete" buttons. They want to show their identity online, and IRL may change with age, but Internet posts will always exist.

The Internet can pose a risk to children. It can also open the door to the miracles dreamed of by previous generations. Help ensure your children's online safety to experience the joys and opportunities of the online world and avoid its harm. Realize. Stay alert. But first, you must actively participate in your child's digital life and daily life, and communicate openly.

Why Should You Teach Cybersecurity to Your Kids?

Now, we understand the importance of security online and in the real world better than ever. The coronavirus disease has forced millions of families worldwide to adopt a social approach and rely on their Internet-enabled devices to talk with the outside world, friends, and family.

As the school locked in for the rest of the semester, students turned to online classes and other ways of communicating with classmates. Not only parents need to adapt to the new home working environment and threatening environment.

The Internet can provide various entertainment activities for children and educational materials, but as children technically surpass their parents, their digital materials can quickly become cybercriminals targets.

The Age Gap in Cybersecurity?

There should be no age deadline for learning good basic knowledge of cyber hygiene. When monitoring which apps and games young children visit, it may be more challenging to focus on young people and their online activities.

More screen time may come at a price. This is why it is essential to teach your young people their digital profile and how they can stay safe while browsing the web-the sooner, the better.

Data shows that three-fifths of children use Internet-based devices at home. It is estimated that children between the ages of eight and eighteen spend about 45 hours a week online, and this number is likely to increase when orders are placed at home Up.

Think Twice Before Posting

We exist in the age of social media, where both adults and children post their daily activities, their likes and dislikes, opinions, daily selfies, and videos.

Some content posted or shared online may be harmless to your young children. However, you should start explaining how the digital world works. Remember, once the picture is online, it will always be online. It is recommended that your kids or teens be cautious about sharing on social media and adjust their profile settings so that only their friends can view their profile.

"Strangers Are Dangerous."

Online popularity and extensive friend lists have become a new boom, especially for teenagers. However, the digital world can also anonymity, and anonymity is often abused by cybercriminals posing as trusted individuals or friends.

It would help when you taught your children to spot red flags in any online communication with strangers. The best practice is to ignore the message request, but it is easy to overlook this step. It is recommended that they be cautious about who they become friends with and reduce some of their risks.

A study by the Center for Cyber Security and Education shows that 40% of children in grades 4-8 talk to strangers online. Even more worrying is that 53% of people provided their phone number, 30% sent text messages, and 15% tried to meet strangers.

Cyberbullying

Cyberbullying can have severe psychological effects on children. The most common tactics include posting vile comments, spreading rumors, threatening, or even impersonating people using fake accounts to damage online reputation.

Social media bullies have caused severe damage, and your child should feel comfortable enough to discuss with you anyone who might harass them online. Help your children pay attention to their practices and immediately report bullying to online platforms or local authorities.

Excessive Sharing and Cyber Theft

Your kids need to worry about more than just online accounts. According to a report by Trans-Union, approximately 20% of children aged 13 to 18 have credit cards. Ensuring they shop responsibly (only on trusted websites) can prevent them from becoming identity theft or fraud victims.

It is recommended that young people not store credit card information when shopping online or make any in-game purchases. If your teenager can access his social security number, please do not force him to provide this personally identifiable information online.

Child identity theft is not a game. According to a 2017 study conducted by Javelin Research, the identities of more than 1 million children were stolen, and 66% of the victims were under the age of 8. The essence of children is more attractive to cyber crooks. Why? It allows criminals to open up new lines of credit, which may be restricted for many years. If your child grows up and wants to apply for a school loan or rent an apartment, he will not repay the loan due to a damaged credit score.

Protect Online Accounts

Most teenagers already have an email account and do not need parental guidance when registering. You should understand the dangers of phishing emails and the importance of protecting your personal information. Therefore, please encourage your child not to click on suspicious links or open attachments he received from unfamiliar email addresses.

You are not only protecting the private information of the account owner but also ensuring that no malicious actions affect devices that other family members may be using.

For online accounts, having a secure password is essential. Most children play online games and set up accounts to allow them to interact with other players. However, the risk of data leakage is not limited to financial accounts. Any user database is useful for cyber thieves.

Instruct your young people not to reclaim passwords and enable two-factor authentication methods when possible.

In the digital age, protecting children's online identities is of utmost importance, and becoming a digital home is difficult. However, long-term benefits are worth the effort. Use the latest security solutions to keep your devices up to date and share your wisdom with friends and family.

Why Teaching Children About the Importance of Cybersecurity and Privacy

Advances in technology have redefined the way of life of our generations. With simple access to the Internet, we can now easily stay safe and work comfortably at home. Educational institutions have also turned to online learning in response to the continuing pandemic. People of all ages rely on smart devices and online applications as never before. Therefore, the vital awareness of the Internet is more critical than ever.

Although the IT departments of most organizations take measures to protect their business data and frequently hold meetings to educate their employees on the importance of network security, the children in our family are often monitored or monitored. Children lack a complete understanding of online safety and the potential risks involved in cyber-attacks. More than three-fifths of children have access to the Internet, and they spend more than 45 hours online every week. With the Internet becoming an essential part of childhood, there is no better time to talk about Internet safety than now, and we have some Internet safety tips to help you get started.

Build Cybersecurity Awareness

Mobile devices or the Internet have become a standard and tangled part of today's children's lives, so they must be taught privacy, computer security, and social media security at a very young age. Please give them a brief introduction to cyberbullying, phishing, cyber threats, and their impact.

Protect Their Equipment

If you and your child share a common computer at home, you must update the system with the latest upgrade. This can improve the device's security and protect your personal and financial information from any imminent cyber threats.

Talk to Them About Privacy

The temptation of online games and social media usually attracts children. Remind them not to share personally identifiable information or financial details with online applications or services, and teach them the difference between security and malicious applications.

Popular social media services such as Facebook, Instagram, and TikTok require users to be at least 13 years old to register. However, there are still many underage users joining. Talk to your child about the impact of sharing sensitive information on social media and the risks of interacting with strangers online. When you want to monitor your child's online activities, please use parental controls on their mobile device.

Use Strong Passwords

Passwords are the first line of defense for any account and must not undermine its security. Encourage your child to use complex passwords, including symbols, numbers, uppercase, and lowercase letters. Please add it to your family's password manager account to help them generate and remember a strong password.

Restrict Access from Public Networks

The appeal of using free Wi-Fi in public places may excite children with limited data. However, a potential attacker can steal data transmitted over an insecure network. Instruct your children not to access sensitive information, or even to access sensitive information completely, to avoid connecting to such networks.

Take Them Offline

Guarantee your kids have a great time on the screen to prevent them from becoming addicted to the Internet. Limit their screen time or encourage them to spend some time outdoors, reading a book, or creating creative ideas.

Why Is Cybersecurity So Difficult?

Cybersecurity is difficult. Ask anyone at the scene, but don't ask what you think. If your Cybersecurity is good, it will be boring. It needs to be strengthened a lot, but it needs to be repaired a lot. (Too many patches.) Although you don't want it to be exciting. Protecting your network assets is not an easy task because the purchases to be covered are not clearly defined and cannot be realized until discovered. It sucks.

First, You Need Protection

This is not an exaggeration. Your family has an internet connection, website, email access, customer portal, etc. All these systems are connected somehow, which means that if one system is vulnerable, they are all. Most importantly, the ground area of your home is open to the outside world. Your customers can access it, which means other people can also access it.

Setting reasonable limits on users is an excellent first step. But more importantly, train family members in basic safety practices. I hope it can withstand basic attacks, and they will know what to do if something goes wrong.

It is essential to plan the environment and record it accurately properly. After all, if something goes wrong, you want to know exactly what you are using. You should pay attention to key services, such as servers, network switches, and storage devices, and set up daily, weekly, and monthly inspections. Items such as log files or network activity should be carefully reviewed so that you can recognize patterns. Once you understand what the baseline looks like, it's easy to spot any abnormalities.

It's You and The Network

There are countless malicious entities on the Internet destroying systems like yours to make a living. Unlike you, they don't have to follow best practices. Your knowledge of Internet security at least matches that of potential hackers. Your skills should also be up to date, covering all the latest changes in information security.

The apparent solution is continuous training, skills development, and skills transfer at home. Comprehensive training will enable your family to work more unitedly in the face of cyber threats.

You Cannot Predict What Will Happen

Hackers and cybercriminals will not send meeting requests or ask permission before attacking the network. Therefore, you realize that the chance of an attack is almost zero before the attack begins. Even if you have performed due diligence, you may still find information about the attack afterward.

The exchange of fire from this unpredictability is part of what makes cybersecurity so challenging-not fully prepared. Therefore, it is essential to track the process through log file analysis and real-time monitoring systems.

Your family wants to take a proactive approach to anything that may happen and outline what to do in this situation. The practice method will confirm that you can recover in the shortest possible time, even if you cannot see it.

Things That Seem to Be Rare Can Become A Big Problem

Many system administrators feel guilty about ignoring Kill messages and failure notifications, especially if they come from non-critical systems or older hardware. These seemingly harmless killings can be the starting point for an attack. An open, unmonitored system allows intruders to enter without resistance.

Once you know what to deal with, you will need to take a proactive attitude and develop a plan to solve these deadly problems. These problems are very similar to seeing a dentist: the longer you leave, the worse the situation.

This Is Not Only Related to Your Safety but Also Your Family

If the scenario we have outlined so far sounds like something you would never do, that would be great. However, you may not only be responsible for everyone's actions.

Tell the family that password complexity and password security play an important role in keeping the environment locked. A small mistake in password processing can cause severe headaches.

Training Everyone Is the Key

When defending against attackers, time is a factor, so training your family to be proactive and alert for any suspicious activity may make a difference.

If the child finds anything wrong, he should contact his parents immediately. This is the best practice for your family.

The only real way to keep up with cybercriminals is to certify and train on the latest technology. With the development and change of technology, you should also understand how to protect the security of your home IT environment.

How do cyber attackers target family and children?

Due to the COVID-19 pandemic, millions of students can study at home, so cybercriminals have shifted their focus to using applications that Australia's 3.9 million students rely on.

Microsoft's Office 365 (O365) software (SaaS) tool has become a must-have productivity suite for many schools and universities and has become a viral target.

Trend Micro recently reported that it captured more than 868,000 high-risk emails targeting 210,000 O365 users last year. I hope it will get worse.

Cybercriminals are also paying attention to the explosive use of school and work-centrist video collaboration platforms (such as Zoom and Microsoft Teams), using new and old vulnerabilities to lock down the digital space where users now work-study.

Authorities have warned that cybercriminals will target virtual private network (VPN) tools used by remote workers and students for secure login-but "many companies are simply not ready to attack this vector," Attivo Networks chief crook Carolyn Crandall Pointed out.

She said: "Using VPN split tunnels to separate home and company traffic, remote workers will not have existing network protections, such as Web filtering, firewalls or intrusion detection systems."

"The attackers will target users who use unmanaged systems to access the company's network and SaaS applications, and will try to compromise those systems that require security updates."

Safety Crash Course

Escalating cybercrime attacks have allowed parents who had been over-expanded to add chief security officers to increase their job title roster – forcing many people to take crash courses on cybersecurity while striving to maintain a strict family study schedule. They tease students about finding learning tools and entertainment online.

Even during downtime, email security company Proofpoint recently pointed out that Australian students eager for entertainment have been hit by malware, credential phishing, and password stuffing attacks-selling streaming credentials in underground markets.

Statistics show that the number of registered phishing websites has increased by 350% in recent months. The threat has become so hard that the World Health Organization is concerned about this situation.

Given the fundamental importance of continuous online communication and the increasing amount of time spent online during the pandemic, which warns that "as the time spent online increases, the risk of the Internet will inadvertently increase. Obtaining obscure websites or pirated programs opens the door to possible malware and attacks."

Learn About Malware

Many students unknowingly introduce malware infections by downloading digital versions of classroom materials, which are usually unsolicited by crooks who take over peers' inbox.

A recent analysis by Kaspersky Lab showed that the company's tools had blocked 234,000 downloaded papers and 122,000 textbooks from potential infections, including English (up to 2080 download attempts), mathematics (1213 times) and literature (870 times) is the most frequently downloaded file.

Kaspersky researchers found that the most common target of infection for digital resources is Stalk. This self-spreading worm can spread on local networks and emails, which are very productive infection vectors in school environments.

Students are also flocking to resources related to COVID-19, which makes them more likely to respond to the surge in the number of phishing emails on coronavirus.

Proofpoint research found that corona-virus-related phishing baits currently account for more than 80% of all malware. Among them, 500,000 emails contain more than 300,000 malicious URLs, 200,000 malicious attachments, and more than 140 different phishing activities.

The Australian Cyber Security Centre (ACSC) has been following the surge in cybercrime related to COVID-19. Acting chief Karl Hanmore pointed out that there are reportedly 1 million Australian dollars in scam losses every day and warned families to "keep cyber vigilance, but don't suffer. Internet alert." These rebates do just that, and they are just recovering our money. "

However, as many Australians have begun to tire of isolation and turn to digital channels for entertainment and communication – increasing usage forces Netflix and YouTube to reduce bandwidth consumption, Microsoft and Sony are shifting multi-gigabyte game downloads to off-peak hours – Students and their parents must be alert to the increased possibility of being harmed or deceived.

The WHO warned: "Cyber-attacks make it impossible for organizations or families to access their equipment, data, or the Internet. This can be devastating or even fatal."

Facts About Internet Safety for Parents

Unfortunately, online is dangerous, and both children and adults must take precautions when using the Internet. Parents need to be cautious and pay attention to safety. They should also monitor their children's Internet usage to prevent abuse or identity theft.

Early Internet Use

In a survey of 825 adults or children between the ages of 6 and 16, Shared Hope International found that one in eight parents allowed their children to use the Internet from two. Therefore, according to expert advice, one in ten children can only wait until they are ten years old or older.

Unsupervised Use

As a result, many children use the Internet unsupervised at an early age. The study found that more than 71% of parents did not supervise their children's Internet use after 14, but in all cases of missing children online, an alarming 72% involved children over 15 years old.

Hide Information from Parents

Unfortunately, regardless of parental intentions or involvement, the Children's Safety Foundation reports that nearly 32% of teenagers hide or delete their parents' browsing history. Parents must be diligent. Similarly, 16% of teenagers have email or social media accounts that their parents do not know. Usually, children will even lie about their age to create such reports, thereby attracting older children and even adults.

Sexual Predator

The National Center for Missing or Exploited Children reported that 15% of children between the ages of 10 and 17 had been contacted via the Internet for sexual intent. These lawyers are likely to be sexual predators. Adults or children need to use the same precautions as online when facing strangers. According to the Associated Press, the authorities have discovered and removed more than 90,000 sexual predators from MySpace's substantial social networking site, which was once popular among teenagers. Most of these predators have been tried, convicted, and imprisoned.

Sexual Plea

Contrary to popular belief, children or teenagers are more likely to be attracted online by their peers. The majority of these linear deception activities are men between 18 and 55 years old. As mentioned earlier, its victims are almost always willing to meet with these predators. About 26% of linear criminals use the information posted on the victim's social networking site to find the victim's exact whereabouts.

With the development of the Internet, the demand for sex with minors has also increased. A survey conducted by the Santa Clara City Sheriff's Office in California shows that online sex scam activities increase at a rate of 1,000% per month! This is another important reason that is; individuals must not disclose their whereabouts and contact information.

Stranger's Friend

Typically, teenagers and sometimes adults are Facebook friends and have online conversations with individuals who have never met. Teens are trusting-often, willing to complete strangers. A recent study found that 16% of teenagers had considered meeting with someone chatting online, while 8% were meeting someone.

Public Social Media

A recent study found that only 62% of teenagers' Facebook accounts are set as private accounts. All public information (including contact information and whereabouts) reached a staggering 17%.

Clear Photo

Research shows that one in seven teenagers took nude or semi-nude photos of themselves, and more than half of them were shared with others via the Internet. It is important to note that once something goes through the Internet, it cannot be deleted.

Online Bullying

There are several anonymous conversation applications and sites where individuals can ask questions or post information to others. These anonymous apps are very dangerous because they promote bullying. An anonymous bully hiding behind a computer screen can quickly mock, mock, and put down other people.

Believe it or not, adults, especially the elderly, are vulnerable to cyberbullying, as are children or teenagers. It is essential to never respond to threatening or obscure information and always be diligent and report any suspicious or proven abuse.

Identity Theft

Children are more victims of identity theft than known. Compared with adults, children under 18 are 51 times more likely to be stolen. Criminals target children because they have a clean credit history and, as mentioned earlier, often publish personal information publicly. Criminals can sometimes use the identity of an unsuspecting child without being noticed for years.

Network Attacks

Internet safety is of utmost importance to both adults and children and young people. In a recent survey, one in ten adults who use social media claimed to be victims of a cyber-attack. Security and antivirus software must be installed on all computers (especially those that store personal information).

Cell Phone

Mobile phones are good for keeping in touch and emergencies. Many parents buy mobile phones for their children. Approximately 69% of young people aged 11 to 14 own a mobile phone. All mobile phone users need to be aware that the GPS of the mobile phone can provide others with the user's exact geographic location. Also, please always be cautious when posting personal phone numbers online.

Web Surfing

Be vigilant when surfing the Internet. Web usage and history are always tracked. Visiting unsafe or inappropriate websites may harm your personal and financial information or damage your computer. Likewise, all computers must have security and antivirus software installed.

Online Shopping

There is no suspicion that online shopping is more attractive than ever because of its convenience and affordability. According to "Business Insider" report, in 2014, 78% of the population over 15 years old in the United States shopped online. Cybercriminals have learned to take the help of this convenience. Before placing an order online, you should always use a secure connection, do not use public computers, and ensure that the website is legal and safe. Following these precautions will provide shoppers with a safer experience.

Video Games

In recent few years, video games have come a long way. With many gaming options available, parents need to know that most gaming devices can connect their children directly to the Internet and other players. Fortunately, most gaming devices have parental controls and security settings. These settings allow restricting access, restricting audio chat, and allowing you to choose who to play. Parents should also narrow the time their children spend playing video games.

Teach Students the Importance of Cybersecurity

The Internet is a necessary part of everyone's life today, including children. And assume that mature, smart, and sometimes even tech-savvy adults can commit fraud online. In this state, we are almost sure that a child full of curiosity but limited maturity and awareness may become a victim of Internet danger. Parents need to keep their children safe online, but it's also helpful if the teacher is involved in the conversation.

Children take technology classes, browse the network of school projects, and use the Internet to handle various things in their free time. Therefore, it is a great idea for teachers to include some knowledge of network security in their courses.

The truth is that cybercrime has become more threatening than traditional crimes. In the past ten years, crimes such as burglary, theft, theft and even violent crimes have been significantly reduced, because criminals have found a new way to break into our houses through our screens, giving them far greater access rights. Far beyond the house or what we can see. Pocket.

In addition to theft, we also need predators to worry about.

Digital Natives

Therefore, please consider the children of today-most children were born in this digital age, and there has never been a world without the Internet. They see the Internet as a huge thing, which contains a lot of information and answers to everything. Hence, they must be made aware of the flaws of the Internet. People with bad intentions will infiltrate the cracks if they are not paying attention and obtain the shots and their personal information.

Cybersecurity in The Classroom

Some schools may not start teaching cybersecurity knowledge until middle or high school, but toddlers use tablets as much as teenagers, so they need to know what to pay attention to. For young children, this may not be easy. Fortunately, there are some ways to make it more friendly to children, such as the comic "The Ninja", which is a safe Internet game that allows children to learn while doing, and parents or teachers can easily monitor it.

Most of the way to teach kids about cybersecurity is to follow the real-world rules you guide them and apply them to cyberspace. Don't talk to strangers – don't chat with strangers or accept requests from friends; don't take sweets from strangers – don't get any free prizes from people you don't know, and most certainly won't share you with anyone on the Personal Internet information. It will help if you also teach them to create good passwords instead of using the same password for everything.

Youth and Technology

For teenagers and minors, it may be a good idea to show them some real examples of problems with Internet sharing. Teenagers like to share what they are doing, who they are with, what they are wearing, and more aspects of life on social media. But they usually don't know that anyone can view the content they post-their teacher, their principal, their family. Even if their account is private, children will speak, and they will linger with adults. There are many ways for strangers to directly hack into their accounts and view posts they think are private. Even deleting a post does not sound as good as it seems, because once there is a problem on the Internet, even if the post is deleted, there are some ways to back it up.

Teenagers need to know that from now on, this will significantly affect their reputation in the long run, which involves going to college and job hunting. Future university administrators or employers can turn their brilliant resumes and certificates into "big fat" with a simple Google search because they published something five years ago.

Technical Functions That Constitute Risks

Other essential technical functions may put children at risk, and they should also be made aware of this. GPS and location services can pinpoint their location precisely and warn predators. Posting that they were alone at home or even going out with their family members indicated that the predators were in a vulnerable position or their property. Predators have even discovered ways to invade the computer and spy on others even when the camera is turned off, so it is a good idea to turn off the screen or cover the camera when not in use.

Nowadays, meeting friends online has become the norm. Although this seems to be an exciting way to make friends and build relationships, it should be limited to responsible adults. Minor gatherings with someone you know online can have disastrous consequences, so please tell them to avoid this, but if this is involved, they should never be alone.

You want to be on the side of the students. You want them to know that if there are any problems in cyberspace, they can discuss with you or an adult at school. Remain firm in dealing with the consequences of cyberbullying and inappropriate online behaviour, while also ensuring the safety of students and ensuring that they can talk to you if anything happens. If they do not speak out, then things may escalate and harm them.

Why Parents Must Teach Children About Internet Safety

We know that parenting is developing in this modern digital age. Traditionally, parents warn their sons and daughters of the personal dangers they face, whether it's pickpockets on the street and strangers in the park. However, today, parents face an utterly different challenge-to to ensure the safety of their children on the Internet.

Now, kids of all ages use the Internet every day, everything from Facebook or Instagram to shopping, gaming, or streaming the latest TV shows. As a result, these young people are as likely to suffer cyberbullying as bullying or digital fraud like street pickpockets.

But despite this-and, the never-ending news about cybercriminals, data breaches, and cyber extortion-parents are still used to the Internet and its hidden dangers.

Have Parents Done Enough to Protect Their Children?

A recent NSPCC survey of You Gov of more than 2,000 parents of children between the ages of 8 and 13 showed that parents avoided talking to their children about the need to stay safe online.

This poll shows that although 91% of eight-year-old children use the Internet at least once a week, parents on average believe that nine years old is the right age for children to understand online safety issues.

Even then, many people are still unwilling to take this responsibility. For example, among all parents surveyed, nearly one-third (31%) admitted that if they asked their children about the problems they encountered online, they would like their children more than other adults or siblings.

Also, one in six (16%) said that they are more confident in advising their children to stay safe "in real life" than to live safely online.

Online Education Is More Important Than Ever

Child welfare experts warn that children may miss important online advice and support at critical moments of development, and encourage parents to speak up.

In the NSPCC study, among the 1,000 children surveyed whose parents had talked to them, nearly two-thirds (60%) said they had changed their online behaviour as a result.

Without this kind of parental involvement, children may find that they are more likely to face cyber dangers-they do not have the required skills or knowledge.

"Unfortunately, we know that children up and down in this country (UK) are struggling because they have difficult experiences online," the charity's CEO Peter Wanless commented at the time.

"Thousands of young people contact us about online beauty, cyberbullying, and after browsing websites that encourage eating disorders, self-harm, and suicide.

"We want to help parents realize that for children, there is usually no difference between the online and offline worlds."

Parents Feel That They Have Exceeded the Depth

Another survey revealed that there is a disconnect between parents and children in terms of Internet safety.

ESET reports that although 88% of parents worry about what their children can access online, only a few have taken steps to protect their children's online experience by using security software and parental controls on mobile devices.

This study of 2,000 parents in the United States and the United Kingdom found that 37% of children did not install security software on their phones or tablets, and only 34% of parents installed parental control applications.

When asked, "When your child accesses the Internet through a smartphone or tablet, what do you pay special attention to?" The safety issue comes first.

81% of people think that their children's access to inappropriate web pages is the most troublesome thing; 71% of people say that it's their children who forward personal information to strangers; 61% of respondents think that spending too much on devices Time is worrying.

Many Parents Can Finish Their Work Quickly

Although many moms and dads feel inadequate or upset about explaining online security, there is no need. There are several things parents can do to help their children understand the risks, and fortunately, many things are simple.

For example, parents should force their children to use strong passwords and password managers, and avoid clicking on suspicious links sent via social media or via email.

Young people should also be advised to be wary of entering sensitive information on unknown websites, which may be fake pages created with cybercriminals.

Also, parents should explain the disadvantages of posting "too much" personal information on social networking sites (because attackers can use it for targeted phishing email campaigns).

Children who are victims of cyberbullying should insist on the abuse information they receive and share with their families, schools, and (if necessary) child support groups and the police. They should also use the "block users" and "report users" options on Facebook and Twitter.

Suppose the parents want to go further. In this case, they can ensure that their children's computers have the latest security solutions, run the newest software (to reduce the possibility of attackers exploiting software vulnerabilities), and back up personal files to the hard drive or secure cloud services provided Quotient.

Towards A Safer and Better Future

All of the above is just the tip of the iceberg. When it comes to online safety education for children, there are more parents can do. Some brave moms and dads' children use VPNs (Virtual Private Networks), while others urge their young people to use HTTPS sites for encrypted Web communications.

And, who knows, through the dialogue between parents and children, they may find that their suggestions cause a "sense of security." They not only found interest in this field but also in talent. Fortunately, there are many ways to cultivate this talent.

But to get there, parents need to work with their children to achieve online safety proactively. Starting a conversation is the most challenging part; but after breaking this barrier, everything else is an opportunity.

Ways to Keep Kids Safe Online

As children increasingly become targets of online attacks, parents must take steps to instill certain computing habits and protect their children's equipment. Here are six tips to ensure that children are safe online.

Children prefer to use computer technology and Internet-connected devices more than ever. Unfortunately, the risks associated with surfing the Internet do not wait just because they are young or because of your children. The recent data breaches by toy manufacturer VT and parental information company unknow Kids (last year was one of the most serious data breaches) have exposed children's information and made children's online safety into the world the most concerning issue for parents everywhere.

In the attack on VT, a 21-year-old hacker managed to compromise the security of the toy manufacturer, resulting in the theft of information on more than 11 million accounts. Most of these accounts belong to children, and this attack exposed the children's IP address, history, personal information, and other information about the parents. They can also find out the birthday, name and gender of any child who has an account.

Since the software produced by unknow Kids allows parents to monitor their children's communication and location information, the data breach of unknow Kids exposed more sensitive information about children. In that incident, because the incorrectly configured database was publicly accessible via the Internet, about 1,700 children had information from social media details to GPS coordinates. In theory, anyone can access these children's text messages and their exact locations for at least 48 days. When the researcher who discovered the exposed database immediately notified the company, the incident showed a security risk related to the online collection and storage of children's information.

For parents, these incidents make people's concerns about the safety and privacy of online children the most important issue. Today's parents need to make sure that they are doing everything possible to educate their children on safe online habits and take into account the safety of the devices they use. Here are few ways to help your child stay safe online.

Use A Virtual Private Network
If you want to prevent tracking your location and protect your family members on any network, the best way is to establish a virtual private

network. It will connect your device to a secure remote server and use an encrypted connection to ensure the safety of the data on the link.

There are two main benefits of using a VPN. The first is to block your IP address, which means you cannot track your child's location online. The second reason is that encrypted connections can protect your family's safety on dangerous public networks, so information will not be intercepted. But you may not be able to establish a VPN connection with every toy in your home, you can at least get a VPN connection for your (or their) smart phone, computer, and other everyday devices.

Practice Basic Safety and Health

Your child has a safe online experience first to get a secure online experience. This means that your computer should be kept at its best in terms of security and develop certain habits online. Place a reputable antivirus solution to ensure that your computer is free of common viruses and malware. Other necessary steps include setting a strong password, updating the operating system and all software regularly, and never downloading untrusted materials. You and your children are also trained on how to recognize standard social engineering methods, such as email or social media phishing.

Understand Their Skill Level

If you have a better understanding of your children's performance in computers and technology, you will be able to teach them better how to stay online safely. For young kids or kids who are not familiar with computers, it may be worth getting them to start learning computer toys made by Leapfrog or VT. Once you have confidence in your children's computing experience, you can transfer them to more adult devices with more protection options.

Know They Would

When your child is old enough to chat with people online, then please know who these people are. If they are classmates, relatives or neighbor children, that may be fine, but strangers or people who may pretend to be friends with your child and close to them may be dangerous to your child.

Be wary of people who are cyberbullying or impersonating friends and family – unfortunately, this happens more often than you think.

There are social networks specially designed for children so that they can determine how to communicate online in a secure environment. Different option is to talk to other parents and arrange a pen pal for your child. The more options you give them, the fewer chances they will consider.

Teach Them the Basics Thing

Not matter how old your children are, when they use a computer, they should know some things, such as what the computer looks like when it is not working, simple electrical safety and never reveal any personal information online. (Check the possible results carefully). Show them what safety procedures you run, and explain to your child why they are important. Do the same for everything else that is vital to your computer.

Explain to them that if anything happens, you will not be angry, and if people contact them online, it is not their fault. Mention that even security measures sometimes fail, and it is a bad idea to trust something more than you when using a computer. Make yourself a secure person to talk about computers, and encourage your children to ask any questions they may have.

Use Parent Block

For young children, parental blocking is still useful, keeping them away from illegal content and accidentally discovering dangerous things. Although you can try to buy the program, it may be easier to check if the browser has options available before removing the wallet. When it comes to protecting children, focus and strategy will always overwhelm technology.

If you are worried that the same program or setting may affect you, please try to log in with a different browser from your child or with another account on the computer. In any case, it is a great idea not to give them administrator access to your computer.

No matter how much they want perfect security, no one can expect it. However, in some cases, as long as there are appropriate measures and protections, privacy and security breaches can be prevented. Following these steps and instilling safe computer habits in children from an early age will significantly help to ensure that children are safe online.

Teach Children to Be Smart About Social Media

Most teenagers use some form of social media and have personal information on social networking sites. Many visit these sites every day.

Social media has several benefits, but also many risks and things that children and young people should avoid. If they post content on the site, they don't always make good choices, which can cause problems.

Therefore, it is essential to discuss with your child how to use social media wisely.

Social Media Benefits for Children and Youth

Social media is an important aspect of the social and creative lives of teenagers and children. They use social media to entertain, build and maintain friendships, share interests, explore identities and develop relationships with their families. This is an extension of their offline and face-to-face interaction.

Social media can connect children and young people to global online communities based on shared interests. These may be support networks, for example, for young people with disabilities or medical conditions, teenagers who are attracted to the same sex, or children with specific cultural backgrounds. Or, they may be sites for commenting and sharing content related to specific interests (such as games, TV shows, music, or hobbies).

Your child can gain many other benefits by using social media:

- **Digital media literacy:** Exploring or experimenting on social media can help your child build knowledge or skills to enjoy online activities or avoid online risks.
- **Collaborative learning:** Your kid can use social media to share educational content in an informal or formal school environment.
- **Creativity:** Your child can be creative through profile pages, photos and videos, and game modifications.
- **Mental health and well-being**: Staying in touch with extended family and friends and participating in local or global online communities can give your child a sense of connection and belonging.

The Risks of Social Media

Social media sites can also bring risks. For your child, these risks include:

- Exposure to inappropriate or unpleasant content, such as mean, offensive, violent or sexual comments or pictures
- Upload inappropriate content, such as embarrassing or provocative photos or videos of yourself or others
- Share private information with strangers, such as phone number, date of birth or location
- Cyberbullying
- Exposure to too many targeted advertising and marketing
- Data breaches, such as selling personal data to other organizations.

Dealing with The Risks of Social Media

Talking about the use of social media is the best way to protect children and ensure their Internet safety. Speaking gives you the opportunity to help your child:

- Figure out how they behave and be treated by others online
- Understand the risks of using social media – for example, the risk of being flagged in embarrassing photos taken at a party
- Understand the dangers involved in sharing content or personal information-this includes not only content shared by your child,

but also images of your child shared by others, or posts and images that others have tagged your child

- Know how to deal with a risks-for example; if your children post an identifiable image of themselves, they can reduce the risk by not including any other personal information.
- Understand what people do when they ask for personal information online, be mean or abuse others, post embarrassing pictures of children, or share information that links back to children
- Manage your digital footprint-For example; you can talk about what your children want their digital footprint to say to them now and in the future.

Learn More About Social Media

Social media platforms and features are always changing, so it's best to keep up with the social media used by your child. You can ask your children which platform is popular and which platform they prefer. You can also ask your child to show you how different social media platforms work.

You may consider checking whether your child's social media choices are appropriate for their age. Some social media platforms have age restrictions. For example, to have a Facebook and Instagram account, your child must be over 13 years old.

But it is often difficult to enforce age restrictions on social media because it is easy to lie online. In addition, many platforms do not have specific age restrictions. Other games similar to the online multiplayer environment allow you to interact with people of all ages from all over the world.

Now, some social media platforms have versions suitable for children, such as YouTube Kids and Messenger Kids, which have different security settings, require more parental involvement, and have age-appropriate content. These platforms can help out your child learn how to browse social media.

What About Banning Social Media?

Social media is increasingly embedded in applications, games, websites and even learning environments, so it is difficult to ban it. In any case, even for young children, prohibiting or blocking social media access usually does not help. This is not a good way to teach children how to manage social media risks and perform well on social media.

If you prohibit social media, your kids may be more willing to check them out when they are away. Your child's Internet access outside the home may be difficult to control.

Set Up Social Media Guidelines

Some written guidelines on social media can help your children use social media in a responsible, respectful and safe way and benefit from it. The agreement may be part of the family media plan. If these guidelines include your social media use and your children's use, then you can be a role model. Your guidelines may include the following.

Use Social Media

This may cover the following basic knowledge:

- When can you use social media and how long your child can spend on social media?
- Is it possible to use social media during homework, family meals, etc.
- Where social media can be used, for example, only in the family area of the house, not the bedroom.

Post Content and Comments

Your child must agree that the following points are important:

- Do not upload or share inappropriate messages, images and videos of themselves or others.
- Be cautious about the information they share.

- Become a responsible digital citizen by showing respect in posts and when sharing content – for example, if it's not okay to say or do something in person, then it's not okay online.

Privacy Protection

People have been worried about how large social media platforms like Facebook handle user data. It is best to read the privacy guidelines and settings together with your child and make a joint decision on the platform and privacy settings the child uses.

Your child can protect his privacy by agreeing to the following:

- Do not share private information such as phone number, location and date of birth with strangers online or with people they don't know.
- Don't add personal details such as phone number or birthday to your profile.
- Check privacy and location settings regularly, especially on mobile phones.
- Keep the password and login details confidential and do not share with friends.
- Log out after using a public computer.
- Disable features, such as posting to multiple social media sites at once.

Stay Safe on Social Media

Your child's safety tips include:

- Block and report people, they don't know or who post unpleasant comments or content.
- Don't click on the pop-up window. Some seemingly safe pop-up windows may lead to pornographic websites or requests for personal or financial information.
- Only accept friend requests from those people your child knows who they are.

- Take screen shots and discuss unpleasant things they see or experience online with trusted adults.

Worries and Consequences

In addition to issues such as cyberbullying and online predators, children may also face the possibility of physical encounters with the wrong people. Many newer applications will automatically display the location of the poster when in use. This can tell anyone exactly where to use the application.

Photos, videos and comments posted online usually cannot be retrieved once posted. Even if young people think that some content has been deleted, they may not be able to delete it from the Internet completely.

Posting inappropriate photos can damage the reputation and cause problems years later; for example, when potential employers or college admissions officers conduct background checks. Moreover, even if it's a joke, sending a vile text can cause significant harm to others, and even be seen as a threat.

Spending too many times on social media can be frustrating again. Seeing how many "friends" other people have and their happy photos may make children feel sad about themselves, or as if they are sorry for their peers.

What Can Parents Do?

It is essential to understand what your child is doing online. However, snooping can alienate them and undermine the trust you build together. The key is to stay involved so that your children understand that you respect their privacy but ensure their safety.

Tell your child that the following points are essential:

- Be nice to people. The average behaviour is abnormal. Make it explicit that you want your children to be respectful of others and do not post harmful or embarrassing messages. Ask them to forever tell you about any harassment or bullying posted by others.

43

- Please think twice before clicking "Enter". Remind young people that the content they post can be used against them. For example, letting the world know that you are on vacation or mailing your home address may give robbers a chance to strike. Teenagers should also avoid posting specific locations and phone numbers for parties or events.
- Pay attention to "WWGS?" (What would grandma say?). Teach children not to share on social media anything they don't want their teachers, college admissions staff, future bosses, or even grandma to see.
- Use privacy settings. Privacy settings are required. Check them together to make sure your child understands each child. Also, please indicate where the password can prevent identity theft. They should never share with anyone, even boyfriend, girlfriend or best friend.
- Don't "become friends" with strangers. "If you don't know them, don't be friends with them." This is a simple, safe and straightforward rule of thumb.

Signing the Contract

Consider signing a "social media agreement" with your child, which is a real contract they can sign. In this agreement, they agreed to protect their privacy, consider their reputation and not disclose personal information. So, they also promise not to use technology to harm others through bullying or gossip.

In turn, parents agree to respect the privacy of teenagers while striving to be part of the social media world. This means you can "become friends" and observe them, but don't make embarrassing comments or complaints about the chaotic room.

Parents can also help children stay in touch with the real world by restricting media usage. Put the computer in the common area of the house, avoid using laptops and smartphones in the bedroom, and make some rules for the use of technology (such as no equipment on the dining table).

And Don't Forget: setting an excellent example through virtual behaviour can significantly help children use social media safely.

Children's Entertainment and Safe Social Network

When your child is on Facebook or MySpace, at least it should not be legal. The Children's Online Privacy Protection Act (COPPA) prohibits websites from collecting personal information about kids under the age of 13 without the authority of their parents.

Many children can bypass the law by simply adjusting their birthday, even on websites that enforce the law. According to recent research conducted by the Kaiser Family Foundation, 75% of students in grades 7 to 12 surveyed said that they have personal information on social media sites.

Children want to use social media, and evidence shows that even though COPPA or many reasonable parental fears have led to social media use, they still do. However, parents can make the experience safer by directing their children to one of these five age-appropriate social networks.

Togetherville

Parents can register their children by creating a profile for their children on their Facebook-like websites using their Facebook accounts. After parents select friends for their children by searching for other children among other students in their children's school, adding family friends from their own Facebook profiles and sending email invitations, the children can access selected YouTube videos, games and creative projects. The website also has other functions similar to Facebook, such as "love it", the function of using virtual currency to buy and send gifts (the difference is that parents give money to their children for free as a "permit") and share Videos and their friends browse other parts of the site.

The separation of the site from Facebook disturbs many parents: no external links, no unapproved friends and no private conversations. To post the original comment instead of the default option, the child must agree to the following code of conduct: "I agree not to say anything mean or hurtful, not to be embarrassed to myself, my friends or family, and to take responsibility for my remarks in Togetherville."

Togetherville's target age is under ten years old, which makes the preset annotation options such as "Hampsters so cute!" understandable. The website also encourages parents to participate in their children's introduction to social media by encouraging parent-child interaction. Parents can not only view their children's social network activities, but they can also post messages on his or her wall, assign "virtual subsidies" and send virtual gifts.

What's What

This website may be the safest social network for children on this list. To sign a contract with a child, parents need to submit their credit card information to verify their identity and must provide the child with three headshots (taken with a camera) for the website to record. As with every position in this list, I can still create an adult profile, so I can browse friends in "My Grades", which I chose as the seventh. However, unlike other websites, the What's What team discovered my adult within about six hours (though these photos) and blocked my profile.

Although children are free to interact with people they don't know, they cannot make friends with people outside their age range (people who are in their grade or lower or higher) without their parents' permission. Also, the function of this network is very similar to other systems: users can exchange messages, make friends, join or create groups, and view friends' personal information. Parents can edit or delete their children's faces at any time and monitor all content posted on the website.

The expected age of the site is between 8 and 14, which seems realistic considering that it retains the functions of the two primary social networks-the ability to "make friends" with new friends and share your ideas with others.

ScuttlePad

To register for ScuttlePad, children must provide their birthday, favorite colour, name, and parent's email address, and they can't use it on the website until their parents approve. After logging in, they are free to post messages, make friends, upload photos and leave comments-but be careful. All comments on the website must follow the given format and use the given set of words. The message is composed of "I click, click, click" in the frame, and each click will cause a word to be selected. Picture are manually approved by ScuttlePad, and only names are used on the website.

The comment outline function makes the website more secure. Anyone of any age and any malicious intention can register, but it is difficult to cause significant losses using the preset communication options. Similarly, it is impossible to bully or even harm anyone by using preset options.

On the other hand, this function can be limited to the extent that it dulls the online experience of older children. The website aims to explain how to use social media sites to children aged 6 to 11, and achieves this goal. However, for young people of that age, this may be the most attractive.

GiantHello

Parents can verify their identity and sign GiantHello for their children by providing the last four digits of their social protection number or by charging a penny to a credit card. The site also provides a social networking experience that is closest to mainstream social media networks, making it more attractive than older children who wish to have greater autonomy on other sites.

The profile page functions much like a Facebook wall:

- Friends can post comments.
- Children can update their status.
- Their page reports activities on the website (such as joining a group).

Children can also choose to send private messages, upload photos, and join fan pages of celebrities (such as Jonas Brothers and Ryan Seacrest), which are updated via the celebrity's Twitter feed.

As far as the social media experience is concerned, GiantHello has cancelled the "search for friends" function, thus separating from its mainstream competitors. Children need to invite friends via email or print it out on a page with the invitation code. Therefore, they cannot make friends with people they don't know.

Skid-E Kids

Most of the safety features of Skid-e's children rely on the staff moderator. If the comment is flagged by the filter as inappropriate language or reveals personally identifiable information, it is sent to human review. The moderator checks all photos; users edit the articles and stories in the "written by you" section to edit inappropriate language and personal information before publishing them and then review the interest group page.

Unlike most sites, parents and children are encouraged to create profiles on the same network. Users can exchange messages, update their status, upload videos (must be approved before posting videos). They can compete against each other in any free game on the website to get high scores. Unfortunately, most of these games start with advertisements, and although they are advertised as educational advertisements, it is difficult to see how things like "Powerpuff Girls Coloring" fit this description.

The advantage of this site, especially for older children, is that the site itself provides a large number of audits. Parents don't always have to sign in or approve decisions but can focus on interacting with children on the same network.

Teach Children to Be Smart About Chat Rooms

A chat room is a place on the Internet that may cause a lot of fears and worries from parents. Regarding the results of the chat room, there are many stories of terrible things happening to children and others, and the concerns about this are understandable.

Finally, children are not recommended to use chat rooms. Online predators and identity thieves lurking in chat rooms and posing as young and friendly have endless potential. Whenever you choose to allow your child to visit them, here are some chat room tips that can help you ease your fear:

Service Host

There is almost always a moderator in any chat room. Their responsibility is to ensure that the conversation stays within the guidelines set in the meeting room and that anyone who violates the rules is removed from the chat room. Internet security starts with these people. Chatdanger.com provides this useful tip to ensure you stay safe in the chat room,

See how to host a chat and carefully consider who the host is. The host can trust the user.

Block and Ignore

In almost every chat room, there is a feature that allows members to block and ignore users who are bothering them. This feature is already in place, so you can ignore specific members and no longer have the opportunity to annoy other members. This is an important function used when someone is harassing your child at the first sign.

Child-Only Chat Room

There are chat rooms, specially opened for children online. They are more strictly monitored than other rooms and may not allow certain types of language or pictures to be sent. In theory, these rooms can only accommodate people of the right age who are talking to your child. However, because it is the Internet, it is easy for adult adults to create accounts under the guise of different ages. When children visit chat rooms for children, parents should be vigilant, even more.

Watch Out for Your Child's New Online "Friends".

Keep an eye on any new friends and followers your child connects with on social networks. Chat room predators try to win the trust of children and may become friends with them on other networks to gain their trust further. Connect with targets on social networks to make predators or thieves look more legitimate. With the help of tools such as unknow Kids, you can master new social network interactions.

How to Ensure That Your Child Can Safely Be Online from Hacker?

Our children grow up in a digital society. With a single click on the Internet, our children can get more information and entertainment than when we grow up. But between funny cat videos and Instagram posts, the Internet is a dark side beyond our control.

Strangers, predators, hackers and cyberbullies all target children, and every year, let them contact our children more comfortable. So, what should parents do? Here are five quick tips to help you keep kids safe online:

Talk Publicly About the Dangers of The Internet

Children use the Internet for all operations. Research by the Family Online Safety Institute (Family Online Safety Institute) showed that 45% of the children surveyed could use three or more Internet-enabled devices. From homework to chatting with friends to playing games, they can easily manipulate every corner of the Internet.

But most of them don't understand the dark side of the Internet, and strangers can hurt them by surfing the Internet as quickly as on a dark street at night.

Once they are old enough to browse the Internet on their own, there must be a public discussion about Internet security. Teach them safety tips or such as not sharing personal information such as phone numbers and pet names with others. Please encourage them to disclose what they do on the Internet.

If they find inappropriate content, such as cyberbullying or harmful comments in explicit videos, you will want them to share with you. Having a clear conversation with your child as early as possible will help ensure their safety.

Use Parental Controls

When you set obstacles, children are very good at finding solutions. However, as children become smarter and smarter, this technology also becomes smarter, and there are a lot of resources such as Clean Router, Content Watch Net Nanny and Custodia Parental Control, which will help you control your children's online behaviour.

Only about half of the parents surveyed by FOSI use parental controls to prevent their children from accessing certain online materials.

These tools allow you to monitor every device on the network, set up safe search enforcement and device-specific Internet scheduling. Subscription services are beneficial and can help you manage your child's online time.

Another useful tip is to use the parental controls built into your Mac, PC or mobile device. Just search for "Parental Controls" and the name of the device or operating system used to follow the instructions.

Set Limits

Children are brought to the screen much younger than before. A report by Common Sense Media found that children under the age of eight spend an average of 2 hours and 19 minutes on-screen media.

Setting a limit on the screening time for young children will better help children make wise choices as they age.

The shorter time a child spends online, the less likely it is to have trouble surfing the Internet. Setting limits, such as no screen time during meals or before going to bed, or a daily screen time limit, can help you control your child's online behaviour.

Another useful technique is to turn screen time into a productive activity. Please assist them in using the Internet to learn, create or build new things.

Check Your Child's Online Activities Regularly

Three out of ten parents (29%) allow their children to use the Internet without any restrictions or supervision. Whether it's checking your child's browsing history or monitoring their behaviour on social media, access to your child's device and the account is essential.

Your child has the right to use their device, which is a privilege you provide and pay for. Knowing their account password should be a mandatory part of that privilege. Pay close attention to who your child interacts with and how to help better you spot cyberbullying or other inappropriate behaviour issues.

This will help when you are still looking for suspicious activity in your child's history, including account deletion and private searches. (For a tutorial on how to do this on all devices, I recommend that you use Wiki How as a resource.) When you discover unusual behaviour, please draw your child's attention and have an open and honest discussion about how they spend time

Pay Close Attention to The Computer

Installing the home computer in a central location will help you visually observe your child's Internet activities. Such a setting will prevent your children from accessing inappropriate sites because they know that you or your compatriots may walk away.

Another useful tip is to set up rules that require them to use tablets in public areas and leave their phones outside the room at night.

How Do You Keep Your Kids Safe Online from Scams?

Surfing the Internet means that you may be exposed to online scams, and your children may not know anything about it. If you allow them to go online, you must discuss online scams. There are many forms of such scams, including those specifically aimed at children.

Educate Yourself First

The first step in defending your children from online fraud is to educate you about the types of fraud currently circulating on the Internet. One type of scam is a free trial, which claims, for example, to provide a free one-month trial of certain "amazing" products. The beautiful text of these scams includes some clauses stating that you will pay for the product every month (forever) after the trial period.

Other some examples of Internet scams include fake Wi-Fi hotspots; social media or email messages indicating that you have won expensive prizes or should participate in contests to win expensive prizes; and fake pop-up windows that indicate possible viruses and malicious software. The latter scam usually looks like a legitimate antivirus program, but the action you take to "repair" your computer is to get a virus.

Unfortunately, these are just some of the many online scams that exist, so be sure to do your homework.

Learning Signs

Once you feel comfortable about your knowledge of online scams, it is time to pass this information to your children. It is very essential to educate them about scam indicators. Typical signs include.

Mistake

Many Internet scams are full of grammar and spelling errors. When you receive an error message about a "big deal" or contest, even if it comes from a "friend", it may be a scam. However, the wording of many Internet scams is perfect because it is one of the ways that scammers can make emails look legitimate.

Foreign Discount

The news from the "foreign prince" says that you need to help them transfer thousands of dollars, and you have to pay a $150 connection fee to enjoy the money, which is now a classic online scam.

Emotional Manipulation

Manipulating emotions is another common trick for liars. Financial stress, loneliness, or frustration are examples of emotional states preyed by crooks. They may not ask for money, but they will insist on personal information, which is then used to steal an identity.

Talent Search

"Children's Talent Search" is a type of scam specifically aimed at children. These scams may imply that the child has joined a specific model agency or accepted an invitation for a screen test. At first glance, they seem to be true, but they always ask for funds to continue to "cooperate" with the agency.

Scholarship Scam

Another scam targeting children is the scholarship scam. They claim to admit their children's academic performance, but like talent scams, they need to pay a lot of upfront costs.

Communication

When identifying fraud, keep open and clear communication with your child. Emphasize that they should always come to you for any suspicious messages or pop-ups they receive, and regularly discuss signs of online fraud, if your home has a lot of Internet usage. The scammer relies on the innocence of the child, so please consider limiting your online time at home until you are sure that your child knows enough about the scammer.

Sexting and Cybersecurity

For teenagers, sharing photos of friends is fun, and sending provocative photos seems innocent and frivolous. However, sex messages may put your child at risk of public humiliation, social isolation and cyberbullying. You can upload photos to social networking sites, where you can easily share or transfer images.

Talking about the risks of pornography and online communication is a good start, but it's also essential to understand the technology you are using. Your child may use jargon that is difficult to interpret.

Also, read about image-based abuse. A place where intimate, nudity or sexual images are distributed without the consent of the poster or someone is threatening to distribute such photos. Image-based abuse may involve photos or video images and have other names, such as IBA and revenge porn. Anyone who is the target of image-based abuse should know that it is not their fault.

Please educate yourself about the different social media platforms that you already have (such as Facebook, Instagram, Snapchat, and Twitter) and how they work.

Also, you can:

- Talk to your kids about the consequences of sexual intercourse.
- Monitor children's online status, especially social networking sites
- Warn your children about cyber predators, image-based abuse, and images that may fall into the wrong hands
- Give kids clear rules about what they can and cannot do with their phones and monitor text messages.
- If your child receives provocative images or becomes a target of cyberbullying, encourage them to stay open with you.
- Do not let your child meet new friends online without your permission.
- Please remind your children that there is some important information that must not be shared online, including addresses, photos and video clips. Also, remember that social networking pages (such as Facebook or Instagram) are public places, and they should think twice before posting comments and uploading photos and information.

Ways to Keep Kids Safe Online

Internet technology can be adopted as a valuable information resource and learning platform. However, since it is mostly unregulated, it also has its disadvantages. Under the protection of a concept called "digital citizenship", there are a growing number of programs aimed at promoting safe, ethical and responsible online participation.

Due to their lack of experience, children may not understand the risks that they may be exposed online. Below, we provide some suggestions or resources to arm parents, educators, and young people use the Internet safely and responsibly.

Have Frequent Discussions Early

Start discussions about online safety and responsibilities as early as possible, and continue regular discussions. Don't wait for problems to occur. Parents can conduct these discussions at home, and teachers can include digital citizenship in the curriculum. This "two-door approach" ensures that all young people have access to the information they need to stay online.

Monitoring and Age-Appropriate Information

Media smarts (a non-profit digital and media literacy organization) recommends that when children are under eight years old, parents should sit with or near them while using the Internet. Children within the ages of 8 and 13 should use the Internet in public home areas or should be conscious of the potential dangers of the Internet. As age grows and the frequency of Internet use increases, adjust the message about online risks.

Keep Up to Date

Make continuous efforts to understand the child's media usage and the latest information on the various applications and websites that the child is using and visiting. If their discussions fit the specific platform your child spends time on, then they will be most effective. Common Sense Media provides reviews about online games, apps and programs that children are currently using.

Set Boundaries

Just like you set boundaries for their offline lives, set basic Internet rules for your child's growth and maturity, and set specific rules about which websites you can visit, which applications you can use, and what content you can share online. Know whose friends are online and offline. Remind children that if they are unsure, worried or confused, they should always talk to a trusted adult.

Use Controls and Filters

Set up filters to try to block adult content. You can also add parental controls to apps such as Netflix so that your children can only see programs that are suitable for their age. Some websites, such as YouTube Kids, try to ensure a safer online experience for children.

Learn from Kids

Today's children have grown up on the Internet. They may know specific websites and applications better than you, but that's okay. Can you take this opportunity to learn from them? This work will show your interest while also enabling you to determine the potential risks associated with the platform.

Reflect Your Media Usage

Set a positive example for your children, both online and offline, are equally important. Please pay attention to your internet usage and online status and personal data. Children will notice your behaviour and learn from it, so modelling digital citizenship and secure media use are critical. Start home time without equipment to provide opportunities for mutual contact and participation.

To Understand

Not all children are bothered by what they see online, but if they see something that makes them difficult, they may feel embarrassed or frustrated, which may make them reluctant to talk about it. Let your child know that if you don't know what happened, you will be powerless. When your child does talk to you about their concerns or what is happening, try to be understanding, supportive, and sympathetic, and make sure they do the right thing to get your attention.

Don't Overreact

Blame your child or one of their friends, so that everything that happens online may be reduced, and they may seek your help in the future. When children feel that they can ask their parents for help on difficult topics, they are less likely to engage in dangerous behaviours.

Generate "What-If" Scenarios Together

"What if...?" What if you are online or see something that makes you uncomfortable? "What if...?" You post some content and decide not to go online? "If..." Is someone asking you to provide personal information online? Experiencing these situations with your children before anything happens will help them know what to do when they are in trouble.

Prevent Dangerous Behaviour

Your child will be a child, and you will not be able to monitor everything your child does online. This is especially true for teenagers. It is crucial to building their "Tool set" so that they can handle various situations. Before posting online, ask children the following: Is this illegal, harmful or harmful in any way, and does this put my personal information at risk?

Teach Problem-Solving Skills

Although preventing problems is an essential first step, it must also provide advice on how to deal with difficult situations or crises. These are a few of the issues that children and adolescents often encounter and how to deal with these problems. In any case, let the children know that they can come and work with you.

Unnecessary contact with strangers: Block the person and report the person to the website.

Excessive contact with peers or cyberbullying: Collect evidence of harassment or bullying (for example, date, what happened, conversation transcript). Ask the person to stop and not fight back or retaliate.

Being asked to send nude photos or "next page": going through "what-if situations". "What if" the person wants to share my photos with others? Brainstorm and reject sex requests, such as humor.

Receive unwanted hexagons: Please follow the principle of "delete and not repeat": delete text and do not share pictures.

From an early age: the knowledge and skills imparted to children by adult supporters, including parents and educators, will have a positive impact on the decisions they make online and offline.

How Do You Keep Your Kids Safe Online from Cyberbullying?

Cyberbullying refers to the use of technology to harass, threaten, embarrass or target other people. By definition, it happens among young people. When it comes to adults, it may fit the description of cyber-harassment or cyberstalking, which can lead to legal consequences and involve jail time.

Sometimes cyberbullying is accessible to spot-for example, if your child shows you a text, tweet, or response to a nasty, mean or cruel status update on Facebook. Other behaviours are less obvious, such as simulating a victim online or posting personal information, photos or videos designed to harm or embarrass others. Some children report that the sole purpose of creating fake accounts, web pages or online characters is harassment and bullying.

Cyberbullying can also happen by accident. The impersonal nature of text messaging, instant messaging and email make it challenging to detect the tone of the sender-a joke of one person may be an insult to another. Nonetheless, how emails, texts and online posts are repeatedly sent is rarely accidental.

Because many children are not even willing to report bullying to their parents, it is impossible to know how several people have been affected. But a recent study on the rate of cyberbullying found that about a quarter of adolescents were victims of cyberbullying, and about one in six adolescents admitted that someone had bullied someone. In a few studies, more than half of the teenagers surveyed stated that they had been abused through social and digital media.

The Impact of Cyberbullying

Nowadays, bullying is no longer confined to campus or street corners; it can happen at home or school, almost 24 hours a day. The child being picked up may feel that he is always being blown up and cannot escape. As long as children can use phones, computers or other devices (including tablets), they are at risk.

Severe, long-term or frequent cyberbullying behaviours may make both the victim and the bully more susceptible to anxiety, depression, and other stress-related illnesses. In some rare but well-known cases, some children committed suicide. Experts say that children who are bullied are at suicidal thoughts and are at higher risk of attempted and complete suicide.

Punishments for cyberbullies may include suspension from school or expulsion from a sports team. Certain types of cyberbullying can be considered a crime.

Signs of Cyberbullying

Many kids and teenagers who are cyberbullied do not want to tell their teachers or parents, usually because they are ashamed of the social stigma or worry that their computer privileges will be taken away at home.

Signs of cyberbullying vary, but may include:

- Depressed during or after using the Internet or phone
- Very secretive or protective of their digital life
- Withdraw from family, friends and activities
- Avoid school or group gatherings.
- Decline in grades and show anger at home
- Changes in mood, behaviour, sleep or appetite
- Want to stop using the computer or mobile phone
- Feel nervous or upset when receiving instant messages, texts or emails
- Avoid discussing computer or mobile phone activity.

How Parents Can Help

If you find that your child is being bullied online, please provide comfort and support. Talking about any bullying experiences during your childhood may help your child feel less alone.

Let your child know that it is not his and her fault and that bullying affect the victim more than the victim. Praise your kid for doing the right thing by talking to you. Please remind your child that he or she is not alone-many people are bullied at some point. Assure your child that you will solve the problem together.

Let someone at the school (the principal, nurse or counsellor or teacher) know about this situation. Many schools, districts, and after-school clubs have agreements to deal with cyberbullying. These vary by community and state. But before reporting a problem, please let your child know that you plan to do this so that you can develop a plan that makes both parties feel comfortable.

Encourage your child not to react to cyberbullying because doing so will contribute to the fire and make the situation worse. But be sure to keep threatening information, pictures, and text, because these can be used as evidence for the bully's parents, school, employer, and even the police. You may wish to obtain, save and print these screen shots for future use.

Other measures to try:

- Stop the bully. The settings of most devices allow you to electronically block emails, instant messages or texts from specific people.
- Restrict access to technology. Although this is hurtful, many bullied children still cannot resist the temptation to check websites or phone calls to see if there are new messages. Put computers in public places in the house (for example, do not use laptops in children's bedrooms), and restrict the use of mobile phones and games. Some companies allow you to turn off the SMS service at certain times. And most websites or smartphones

include parental control options, allowing parents to access their children's messages and online life.

- Learn about the online world of children. Ask on social media sites to "become friends" or "follow" your child with your child, but don't abuse this privilege by commenting and posting anything on your child's profile. Check their posts and the websites the kids visit and pay attention to how they spend online. Discuss with them the importance of privacy and why even sharing personal information online with friends is a bad idea. Write down the phone and social media contacts you are willing to execute.
- Learn how to keep your kids safe online. Please encourage them to protect their passwords and never post their address or whereabouts while out.

When your son or daughter agrees, you can also arrange for mediation with a school therapist or counsellor who can work with your child and the bully.

Tips to Prevent Kids from Being Cyberbullied

Cyberbullying is more than just "children as children". Although it usually starts face-to-face with people, the victim knows, text and social media can quickly and effectively evolve into widespread harassment and public humiliation. Cyberbullying occurs in many forms, from sending offensive messages or threats, spreading rumours, posting unwelcome pictures or pretending to be others.

Young people require to understand the consequences of their online posting. Sharing personal information through social networks, text messages, or other online activities is an easy way to ensure online security is threatened.

When they later apply for college or work, even joking things may be against them. Moreover, if the speech is intended to harm or harass someone, the sender may violate the terms and conditions of the service provider or social platform. As the laws in each state become stricter, cyberbullies and their parents are increasingly facing legal charges of harassment.

To better protect your children and ensure their safety, please talk to them and learn more about their experiences in cyberbullying. Think these tips as a way to start a conversation and stay safe online.

1. Once your child has a personal phone or social media account, it's time to explain the consequences of posting. Set and retain boundaries. If you post or forward destructive pictures or messages, you will consider losing your phone or computer privileges.

2. Make sure teens know what is online and stay online. Any electronic news can be published quickly. If you don't want everyone to know, please don't send it online. Even better, please follow this proverb: If you are embarrassed to publish it on the front page of a newspaper, don't write it.

3. Encourage your children to tell adults if they see cyberbullying. Let them know that if they are the victim, they will not be punished, and assure them that being bullied is not their fault.

4. If your child is being harassed, please keep all cyberbullying news as evidence. Depending on the severity of the information, parents may wish to involve the school or the police.

5. If necessary, block the person sending the harassing email. You may also be required to obtain a new phone number or email address, and be cautious about who knows more contact information.

6. Make sure that teenagers do not share passwords with anyone other than their parents. Please do not write it down or save it where others can find it.

7. Parents may wish to store electronic products in shared spaces such as a family room and restrict Internet access in their children's rooms. It is also essential to have everyone shut down all technologies at all times. Consider setting boundaries at mealtimes when everyone turns off their phones, tablets, and computers, or at specific times in the evening.

As a parent or guardian, you must pay attention to warning signs that indicate that someone you know is being bullied online. When your kids are a victim of cyberbullying, please record the behaviour and report it to the school or law enforcement immediately.

Useful Tips to Keep Your Kids and Family Safe Online

Children today can access more information than any previous generation. Tablets, laptops and smart devices are expected to be used in schools and homes. Internet delivers a wealth of information that can enrich our lives. But it will also harm our loved ones and us.

You need your children to have access to information, although you also want them to be safe. How can you get these two things at the same time? This is the challenge of living in an interconnected world.

The bad guys may be smart, although you and your children can be smarter. These Internet safety tips can help.

Educate Children

In terms of network security, children are usually one of the weakest links in the family. Teach children about suspicious activities online and encourage them to seek help in the event of an abnormal situation. Install security software to prevent children from clicking on the wrong link and visiting the wrong site.

Remind Children Why Their Identity Is Important

Sometimes children will disclose personal information online, exposing themselves to identity theft because they think they will not lose anything. The identity of a child can be as valuable as the identity of an adult, or more. Scammers can trick children into revealing their social security numbers and other details for identity theft.Remind children not to reveal too many information about themselves. Their date of birth, address or SSN are all personal information, so they should not be shared randomly.

Understand That Private May Not Be Private

As more and more websites and apps collect information and use it for advertising or marketing purposes, make sure your family knows the importance of online privacy. Many applications have privacy policies that stipulate that these applications collect and share information about their users. Children and many adults often accept these policies without seeing them.

Even when your settings are set to private, remember that nothing is private. Even so-called private browsers are not private. Law enforcement, webmasters, and hackers can access what you call private information.

Beware of Phishing

You may be clever enough not to click on the URL of your bank or friend, but does everyone in your family know it? Teach your children about phishing warnings and warn them not to click URLs in emails or social network messages. Install and use a security program that can identify and block unreliable URLs.

Use A Password Management System

For most people, passwords are the primary means of preventing hackers. However, many people reuse the same password in multiple accounts and use passwords that are easy to guess because they are also easy to remember. A password management program can enhance the defence capabilities; the program can remember the unique password of all accounts. Most importantly, with a password manager, you only need to remember one password.

Keep Social Networks Safe

Someone in your family is probably on a social network. But social media can also attract cybercriminals. Pay close attention to your social accounts. When someone has sent you a message that hasn't been sent to you for a while, please stay suspicious. Your best friend's account may have been hacked.

Learn the Importance of Data Backup

Ransomware is very familiar with cybercriminals. They can lock your computer and prevent you from accessing your valuable files, such as private photos and tax information. One of the good ways to combat the threat of ransomware is to back up your data regularly.

Recognize That Network Security Is A Moving Goal

Cybercriminals continue to present new threats. This means that you required to pay attention to download the latest security updates and patches. Let you and your family learn about new ways for cybercriminals to conduct business. Stay up to date and follow news about all major threats.

Don't Give More Information Than Necessary

It is important for children and family members to know how much information is too much. To share their milestones, children sometimes post their personal information online. For example, a driver's license or travel routes shared online can be valuable information for identity thieves and thieves.

Find Other Vulnerabilities in The Home

Your home Wi-Fi network is another entrance point for hackers. Cybercriminals can invade home routers and access various Internet-connected devices, such as home security systems and smart doorbells. Make sure that your home Wi-Fi system has a password that is difficult to crack, and consider security software to identify "intruders" on the network.

Privatization Via Public Wi-Fi

Emphasize the importance of avoiding public Wi-Fi networks. When children connect to public Wi-Fi in shopping malls and coffee shops, they may not think of hackers and cybercriminals. If connecting to public Wi-Fi, always use a VPN, such as Norton Secure VPN.

Don't Forget the Connected Device

Your smartphone or tablet need as much security protection as your PC. The same goes for your thermostat, smart doorbell, home security system and other devices connected to the Internet. Make assured you have a security solution that helps protect all connected devices.

Close Unused Accounts

Unused accounts can become a rich source of personal information for cybercriminals. Sometimes, children create an account using their first and last name or birthday as a username. Cybercriminals can patch these data points together or steal information from other sites used by individuals. If you think you won't revisit the site, it's best to close the account.

If You Have Any Questions, Please Call the Support Department

The best security software programs provide 24x7 support. When you suspect that you have been hacked, please call for help. If you think your device is being attacked by malware, spyware or ransomware, please call for help. A good security kit will have experts to help you solve the problem.

Use A Trusted Security Suite to Protect Your Device

When purchasing a security kit, make sure you purchase software that provides comprehensive protection for all family members and their devices.

How Can I Keep My Grandma and Grandpa Safe Online?

The Internet security of the elderly is the same as the Internet security of anyone else. They require to be educated on how to deal with threats, how to use social media safely, and how to keep their software (especially antivirus programs) up to date.

Primary Online Safety Education for Seniors

Online security starts with education. Older people face the same malware and phishing attacks like everyone else, but they may be more vulnerable because they may lack experience in navigation technology.

Take time to communicate with your grandparents about online safety. Explain that not all online content can be trusted, and they should never disclose personal information such as credit card numbers to online strangers.

Explain Online Scams

Online scams are especially dangerous for inexperienced people. Unfortunately, many scams deserve attention.

Here are a several of the most common online frauds:

- Provision of gifts and prizes
- Advice on discount prescription drugs
- Requests for personal information claiming to be from government agencies such as the Social Security Administration

Introduce these scams to your loved ones and explain that if they have any questions, they should ignore the email and message and let others know immediately.

Helping Seniors Stay Away from Coronavirus Scams

Online scammers see the coronavirus pandemic as an opportunity to profit from uncertain times. They still use the same bait and conversion strategies but make false (and sometimes dangerous) promises such as cheap toilet paper, medical supplies, and vaccines.

So far this year, the Federal Trade Commission (FTC) has received more than 130,000 complaints about COVID-19 scams-scammers have taken $130 million from vulnerable Americans.

The great news is that these strategies are not new, so there are many things you can do to help older relatives discover the coronavirus scam:

- Delete emails purporting to be from "official" sources. Public health organizations do not use email to spread important news.
- Never click a link in an email from an unfamiliar sender. The first information about relief supplies, vaccinations and coronavirus testing is through public health agencies and announcements from national and local news.
- Stop fraudulent calls. Robocall is the most successful scam during the pandemic. Check the FTC's guidelines to block unwanted calls and help set up blocking procedures on loved ones' mobile phones or landlines.
- Be wary of social media. Since March, researchers at the University of California, San Diego have discovered nearly 2,000 fake posts promising to test, treat, and treat the coronavirus. They also found no financial fraud on social media. Older family members are urged to avoid any COVID-19 news, treatment or calls for financial support that are only posted on social media platforms.

Ten Easy-To-Follow Online Safety Tips for Grandparents

Don't Believe Every Email You Receive

Some cybercriminals can impersonate others to steal your personal information. So, how do you know when you were deceived? The simple way to stop this is to avoid talking to people you don't know. You should further avoid clicking on links sent from unknown sources, and never provide your personal information to websites beginning with https://

(you will see a lock in your browser). Also, your bank will nevermore ask you to provide your email address, so please don't disclose it.

Be Wary of Downloading Attachments

If you receive an email from an unknown source with the attachment ".zip", ".rar", ".exe", Word document or seemingly innocent photo, please do not download it. These may contain malicious software that may infect your computer. Be wary of emails from friends, because they will send you malicious software unknowingly. If you do not want to receive their emails, it is best to confirm with them first.

Browse the Web Safely

Don't just provide your personal information to any website without considering why it is requested. You should also trust your browser as if there is anything suspicious, and it will notify you that the site is potentially dangerous. It is best to pay attention to.

Use A Different Password and Make Changes

If you want to register yourself on a trusted website, make sure to use a password that contains letters, numbers, and symbols (although some websites still require you to do this). Nevermore use the same password for all accounts and make sure you change them frequently. Also, please do not send the password to anyone or write it down. This may seem extreme; however, you need to prevent others from accessing your network.

Eliminate annoying ads, until your browser is full of annoying banners, pop-ups and advertisements that you don't want to see, you don't know what innocent clicks can do. To avoid these situations, install a blocking service, such as AdBlock.

Pay Attention To SMS

Cyber attackers are now using this messaging service to conduct attacks, so you should also be alert to the content of these messages. A few months ago, this medium spread a piece of malware that asked, "Is this your photo? -Once the victim clicks on the link, an application that can monitor their contacts is installed on the device.

Install Antivirus Software on All Devices

Let antivirus software take care and protect your device from malicious software, and let the experts worry about your computer or smartphone. They help ensure your safety when shopping online and give you peace of mind when you go online.

Professional Warnings with Public Wi-Fi Areas

Many times, are when you arrive at the train station, cafe or hotel and connect to the free Wi-Fi. Although it is convenient, remember that it is an available connection and you should be very careful when touching. When browsing, please make sure there is a lock symbol and avoid bank transactions.

Delete Your Tracks When Using Another Computer

If you log in to your email account or another service while using another computer, please make sure to delete all browsing history, including cookies. If you are not sure where to find a way to delete a track, follow the simple tutorial in Chrome.

Allow Updating Your Software And Operating System

The old saying "know your devil better" does not apply to the Internet. If your operating system or any installed application says there is an update available, please read it carefully and install it. Even if you need to adapt to some changes, it is best to have the latest version because it will be the version for which the developer has installed the latest security updates.

Teach Safe Social Media Use

The way the elderly use the Internet is changing. Grandparents are increasingly using social media to keep up with friends and family.

Although this is very important to alleviate the social isolation that many experiences with age, it also means that they need to receive education about the safe use of social media.

Here are some social media safety principles that your grandparents need to follow.

- Use appropriate security settings on websites such as Facebook.
- Avoid personal posting of information, such as phone numbers and addresses.
- Before accepting friend requests, make sure they know who someone is.

Set Up Your Computer with Antivirus Software

Install antivirus software on the grandparents' computers and show them how to keep them up to date.

This can help avoid the accidental judgments we all encounter from time to time, which is a worthwhile investment.

How to Protect Your Home Wi-Fi?

Safe Wise tells you how to protect Wi-Fi step by step and keep hackers away from your home wireless network. We will study how to connect to the router, set a strong password and protect all devices using the Wi-Fi network. We even put forward some non-technical tips so that anyone can easily upgrade security.

Step 1: Protect the Router

Your wireless router is like the mother ship of the Wi-Fi network. If the defence measures fail, your Internet connection and every device that uses it is vulnerable to hackers, viruses, and other cyber threats. Use these router security tips to mask and deter attackers.

Start with A Secure Router

Most people use routers provided by their Internet Service Provider (ISP), but this is not always the safest option. Instead, buy a router with features such as guest access and parental control. We recommend using Linksys AC1900, which also includes a firewall and a low price.

Rename Your Network

All routers have a default network name or SSID (Service Set Identifier). Hackers can determine which router you have based on the SSID, which makes your Wi-Fi network more susceptible to hackers. Change the name, just avoid using personal information (such as "Judy's Wi-Fi"), and don't attract destiny with a name like "Unbreakable".

Enable Encryption

There are several types of encryption out there, and their names look like a mess of alphabet soup. Your choices are WEP (Wired Equivalent Privacy), WPA (Wi-Fi Protected Access) and WPA2 (Wi-Fi Protected Access 2). Makes sense, WPA3 is just around the corner. Once the work is done, encryption can protect all data flowing into and out of the network. Today I will use WPA2. It only takes a few minutes (about four steps) to enable WPA2 on the wireless router.

Activate the Firewall

Because you have followed our first technique, you have a wireless router with a built-in firewall. However, only by activating it can it ensure your safety. Firewalls help hide the network from cyber attackers looking for targets. To find the router's built-in firewall, log in to the router's management settings and look for a label or page labelled "Firewall" or "Security." Next, look for an enable button. Click the button, and then click Save or Apply. It's that simple.

Keep the Software Updated

Sometimes I feel that software updates are not suitable for me. But their annoying presence is to ensure the safety of our equipment and information. The same applies to routers. Some routers perform updates automatically, but even in this case, you should set a monthly reminder to check-in to see if any firmware or software updates are waiting for your attention.

Step 2: Use A Strong Password

This is nothing new, however strong passwords are the cornerstone of online security. When setting up a wireless network, you will come up with more passwords to add to your favorites. To control the Wi-Fi network, you need an administrator password. You also need to enter a password to connect to the system.

We know that creating an anti-hacking password is very difficult, and it is almost impossible to remember it. Although you don't have to do it alone. We recommend using a password manager, such as Dash lane. Not only will it store your password, but Dash lane will also generate a secure password, so you don't have to work hard.

Step 3: Protect Devices That Use the Network

Every device connected to and using a Wi-Fi network is a potentially troublesome gateway. To avoid threats as much as possible, please ensure that the machine using the system is not a vector of viruses, malware or hackers. We recommend using the following tools to strengthen wireless devices connected to your wireless network.

Internet Security Software

Even though your computer, phone, and tablet may already have some security features, it is wise to double-process. It attaches an extra layer of protection through third-party Internet security software. The software protects against malware, viruses or other online threats. There are different types of Internet security software to choose from; they can be free or require a monthly (or annual) subscription. To narrow it down, check out our favourite anti-virus and anti-malware solutions.

Virtual Private Network (Vpn)

VPN creates a dedicated tunnel between your wireless network and the Internet. It prevents hackers and other troublemakers from tracking your online activities. It will also hide your system and the IP address from the outside world. VPN is usually a paid service. It sets up a virtual server that will log in every time you go online.

When you are away, please use public hotspots to use VPN. But many experts recommend that you log into the VPN every time you go online. If you want to try a super stealth VPN, we recommend that you use AVG Secure VPN. For about $60 a year, you can enjoy an unlimited number of devices, 24/7 customer service, or compatibility with Windows, Mac, iOS and Android. Also, there is a free trial period.

Parental Control Software

This is a more specific form of online security, but if the kids in your family are very young (or teenagers), then this may be the subtlety of online security. The parental control software can help you prevent children from seeing inappropriate content, and can even monitor social media interactions and be alert to cyberbullying. Most importantly, it usually comes with anti-virus and anti-malware protection-so you only need to buy it once to get multiple benefits.

The overall best choice for parental control software is Net Nanny. It is a pioneer in the industry, has won numerous awards and received positive customer reviews. You can also do it to protect computers or mobile devices, but parental control software is not always the case.

Social Media Guide for Grandparents

Research released this year by online security company AVG shows that Australian grandparents are successfully seeking technology to keep in touching with their grandchildren. We will examine what this research means for grandparents and provide some useful social media tips for tech-savvy baby boomers in the digital age.

The AVG digital diary study of baby boomers and seniors conducted by AVG Technologies showed that half of the grandparents surveyed felt that technology makes it easier for them to communicate with their grandchildren.

How Do Grandparents Use Social Media?

As our families are getting farther and farther away from our homes, 16% of grandparents said that they now spend more time communicating with their loved ones online than face-to-face. However, nearly half (46%) of Australian baby boomers and seniors say they share more with their grandparents than their grandparents.

Grandparents use the following techniques to keep in touch with their grandchildren:

- Email: 41%
- Texting: 34%
- Multiplayer games: 33%
- Video conferencing tools including Skype: 29%
- Communication applications, such as WhatsApp: 5%

As smartphone cameras gradually replace digital cameras, AVG's Director of Security Awareness, Michael McKinnon, said: "Replace Gran's bragging book with videos of every toddler milestone on smartphones and iPads."

Grandparents can help their children and grandchildren safely browse the vast world of the Internet. Respondents said they gave their grandchildren the following advice:

- Don't share too much information online: 50%

- If anything, frustrating happens online, talk to an adult: 46%
- Don't visit dangerous places: 43%
- Remember, everything you post online is always visible online: 43%
- Don't talk to strangers: 42%
- Consider the time you spend online: 40%

British grandparents who use social media could benefit in many ways compared to a control group who did not use social media. Older people who use social media have reduced loneliness, increased self-competition, enhanced personal identity, and even improved cognitive ability.

Social Media Platforms That Grandparents Need to Know

Facebook

Facebook is an application for sharing status updates (stories), photos and videos. In a recent large-scale study conducted in the United States, more than half (56%) of older adults said they liked and liked Facebook the most. On Facebook, you "become friends" with someone to check their status updates and send them messages. You can also "like" pages you like, such as your local lawn bowls club, a charity you support or the "Sailor Man" Popeye.

To make your grandson happy to be your friend, you can:

- Please do not post any cute photos in the bathtub.
- Do not send friend requests to their friends.
- Don't participate in conversations you don't join in.
- Unless you're talking about the same thing, don't comment on other people's things. The news that Uncle Jeff got through the colonoscopy is not a statement of photos of your grandson's pet dog. It is indeed, private news.
- Don't ask all your grandchildren to play with you in Facebook game apps such as Farmville or Candy Crush Saga.
- Don't use your grandchild's baby photo as a profile photo.

- Do not post a vague status, so as not to sound troublesome when you are away (called "fuzzy booking"). When you need to chat, please call.

Twitter

Twitter is an application for sharing status updates, photos and videos. Twitter only allows you to post short updates with a length of 140 characters. Online guides like this, there are some excellent beginner guides. You can "follow" anyone on Twitter, from your grandson to Prime Minister Tony Abbott to the ABC News Service to the sailor man Popeye. Unfortunately, this also means anyone who wants to follow your grandson – so you should urge them to pay attention to their Tweets!

Instagram

Instagram is a photo-sharing application where you can take photos with your smartphone camera, edit it in the application and post online. Although Facebook has always been popular with seniors, almost every teenager you know is on Instagram. You can track anyone you like on Instagram, from your grandson to the sailor man Popeye.

Snapchat

Snapchat is a photo or video-sharing application. The picture you send will disappear in 10 seconds or less and can only be seen by the person you sent it to. Therefore, unless you know his mobile number, you cannot chat with the "Sailor Man" Popeye Snapchat. Snapchat attracts kids who want a more spontaneous "temporary" way of self-expression. However, just like other social media platforms, the content you share will always be available online in some form.

Founder Evan Spiegel (Evan Spiegel) said that Snapchat's goal is to be more private than Facebook. On Facebook, any friend can comment on any content you post. However, more and more privacy poses problems, including the trend of "sending"-sending naked photos of yourself to others.

What Does This Mean to Me?

Before you start worrying about how much your grandchildren are doing online that you might not know, take a breath. Next time you have the opportunity to chat with your grandson to discuss the social media platforms they use and how to use them.

You don't need to teach their knowledge, and you don't need to "Face-talk" every post on their profile. Just questioning them about their social media activities will help them think more about what they post online. You can keep in touch and help them stay safe immediately.

Other apps that your grandchildren may be using include WhatsApp for text messaging, Tumblr and Flickr for sharing videos or photos, and Vine for sharing 6-second videos.

Online Safety for Adults

Online safety is equally important for adults as well as children and young people. From privacy issues to identity theft and online tracking, there are many hazards on the web. Fortunately, some smart moves and specific awareness will go a long way in protecting your Internet.

Major Online Threats for Teenagers

The Internet is a maze, hackers and other cybercriminals may destroy useful information and attractive websites. If it comes to protecting your children, your first line of defence is to understand the twists and turns your teen goes through when entering this tricky environment. Below are the most essential online risks and their impact on your teenagers.

Cyberbullying: There is a long history of fun among young people, but today, this kind of ridicule and abuse does not stop at the door of high school. Social media, email, text messaging and instant messaging (IM) can invade your teen's world 24/7. Sadly, having multiple accounts led to cyberbullying, leading to suicide.

Sex Messages: Whether sending or receiving photos (or provocative jokes), sex messages can cause a lot of trouble. Depending on the distance and whether the exchanged images are confidential, texting may result in severe reputation loss or child pornography allegations.

Identity Theft: When your teenager has no credit or assets to steal, it may seem strange to worry about identity theft. However, cybercriminals like to take away the blank credits of teenagers and open accounts that can follow your children for years. The damage may make it tough for you to complete things like buying a car, renting a house, or finding a job, thereby affecting the future of your youth.

Pornography: Exposure to pornography can have lasting effects and hinder your teen's ability to establish healthy, caring relationships in the future. It generates unrealistic expectations, may affect self-esteem, and confuse adolescents' understanding of romantic relationships.

Online Predators: Online predators often pretend to be peers, trying to establish contact with potential victims. They can appear in social networks, chat rooms and other online environments. Many predators push to exploit or traffic people for young people sexually. However, more and more online predators aim to radicalize children into extreme political or religious groups.

Keep Your Personal Information Confidential

The Internet is full of possibilities to share personal information, but this can leave you vulnerable to identity theft, network tracking, and other problems. According to "Public Opinions on Privacy", 89% of people worry about the level of private information on the Internet.

The following tips can benefit you to stay safe.

Consider What You Share in Your Profile

On social networking sites, a lot of information is usually contained in personal data. From your employer to your religious opinion, please think twice before posting it on the web. Make sure the knowledge you share is suitable for everyone.

Think About the Photos Before Sharing

Sharing photos may be a great way to connect with friends and family, but it can also make you vulnerable. Before sharing the picture, take a few minutes to check the background for details. Make sure you exclude cropped photos that show our residential address, car license plate, and other knowledge that others can use to find you.

Check the Company's Privacy Policy Before Buying

You may have noticed that you start to receive emails and even phone calls after purchase. This can happen when the company shares your information and purchase history with others. Please check the company's privacy policy before making any internet purchases. They should never share or sell your data.

Watch Out for Phishing

Phishing is a common technique used by identity thieves to obtain your personal information. This crime involves sending emails or creating websites that appear to be from legitimate companies and asking you to confirm private information, such as bank account numbers, passwords, date of birth, or address. PayPal and eBay are the two most common targets of phishing scams. Before adding any personal information, please contact the hypothetical website directly to see if they have been trying to obtain your information. Most well-known websites will not contact you in this way.

Attention Account

When you use a credit card for online shopping, be sure to pay close attention to account activity. If you find a purchase that has not yet been made, please contact your card company immediately.

Aware of Your Internet Presence

Everything you do on the Internet is evident to other users, and you should understand what they see. In the case of online tracking and identity theft, someone can use your name and information to create destructive profiles or publish public messages. Take a moment to "use Google" yourself and see what other people think of you. This will enable you to understand any unauthorized use of your name, picture or personal information.

Report Identity Theft

When they think about Internet security, adults most often regard identity theft as a top priority. Identity thieves can use the information they get online to drain your bank account and destroy your credit rating. In many cases, the damage caused by identity theft can even harm your future employment prospects, primarily if you work in an industry that regularly conducts credit checks for all job applicants. When you find that someone else is using your name, credit card or other personal information, please contact the Federal Trade Commission immediately. You can sue this person to clear your name and avoid any further problems.

Keep Your Account Safe

In addition to protecting your privacy, you must also ensure the security of your Internet account. Please keep these tips in mind.

Choose A Good Password

Although choosing a password that is easy to remember (such as your child's name, date of birth, or your favourite sports team) may be tempting, these passwords make you vulnerable to identity theft and fraud. According to Consumer Reports, 32% of adults use passwords based on simple personal information. Instead, it is best to create a password that meets the following conditions:

- Eight or more characters

- A number, and letters
- Unique name, such as %, *, @ or?
- Uppercase and lowercase letters
- No personal information

Do Not Reuse Passwords

To remember your password, you can use the same password for multiple accounts. Avoid this as much as possible, because once a password is discovered, it makes various accounts vulnerable to attack.

Keep the Password Safe

Because you did not reuse passwords, it is difficult to remember all passwords. Many people use the login information of their various online accounts to save lists or files. The safest place to keep this list is an external flash drive that you carry with you.

Watch Out for Keyloggers And Malware

Specific computer programs (called keyloggers) can track the keys you type and transmit this information to people who might want to steal your account. Make sure that you have adequate security programs on your computer, and be extra careful when entering password information on public computers.

Always Be Vigilant

If you are negligent, you may automatically click on links or open email attachments, which may put your computer or information at risk. Being vigilant can help you stay safe.

Think Twice Before Opening Email Attachments

Don't check email attachments from people you don't know. These attachments may contain viruses or other malicious software. Also, think twice before opening attachments from people you know. It's very common for email accounts to be hacked. If it doesn't sound like an email your friend might send you, then the hacker might send messages and attachments to everyone in the address book and send him, or she separately Mails to find out if it is legitimate.

Consider the Legality of Free Programs

Unless you are sure from a well-known company, please avoid downloading free software online. Many free programs are simply devices used to deliver adware and spyware.

Keep Virus Software Up to Date

Install virus protection software and firewall. Check for updates regularly.

Watch Out for Fraud

The global nature of the Internet has injected new vitality into scams. Some of the most common forms of Internet fraud include:

- Goods that do not exist or misrepresented on the online auction site
- Nigerian Money provides promising large amounts of cash in exchange for help with bank account transfers
- A financial scam targeting consumers with poor credit, who are deceived into paying upfront expenses in the hope of receiving a credit card or personal loan
- Phony raffle requires payment to claim non-existent bonus

Vigilant Predator

When you are a single woman who likes to use online dating sites, beware of potential sexual predators. It is not always easy to judge a possible date just because of his appearance or trying to cover up the criminal past. If you do decide to schedule a personal meeting with someone you meet online, always ask that your first date is in a restaurant or similar public place. It's also a good idea to tell your friends where you are going and make sure someone can check on you later in the evening.

Maintain A Pleasant and Safe Experience

If you are aware of the dangers and use the Internet responsibly, it may be an excellent tool for meeting people, sharing experiences, shopping, and gathering information. Remember these tips to ensure that your Internet experience is both enjoyable and safe.

Ways to Protect Your Teen from Sexual Predators

Regrettably, statistics on child and teenager sexual abuse are still growing. This is the worst vision of every parent. Given this danger, can you take some steps to protect your youth? Absolute. Now is the time. Here are five tips for having a conversation with children to discuss how to protect them from sexual abuse. Plan to set down at least one hour of uninterrupted time with your teenager to openly discuss the real dangers of sexual predators and practical steps you can all take to prevent sexual assault.

- Alerts and awareness-always stay alert, especially when outside. If walking to and from school, in a parking lot or even a shopping mall, be attentive to what is happening around you. Try to avoid walking alone after dark. Ask a partner to take you to the car after getting off work. Go to the gym or park with your fitness partner. Identifying areas that are more prone to danger, your teen may find himself alone and suggest safer options. Please note it is no longer just "stranger danger" anymore. Your child already knows that the likelihood of a potential predator is very high. This may be a teacher, coach, neighbor or family friend. Never let your guard down.
- Make a strong sound-if you see something, please say something. Speak out loudly about yourself or other people in danger. Tell potential attackers or creepy strangers in a firm and loud voice, "Stay away from me! Don't touch me!" Attract the attention of passers-by to scare off the attacker. Speak out another person; you are not an easy target. But what if you know this person? What if it is a family member or boyfriend/girlfriend? Once again,

say it out loud with a firm, firm attitude, and then tell your parents or a trusted adult what happened.

- Online danger – You cannot overemphasize the importance of keeping their personal information from predators surfing online to teenagers. Don't simply tell them not to provide any identifying information, but show them examples. Please do not let them leave their mobile phones or devices in the bedroom after turning off the lights. Using social media is a right, not a right, and your children need to abide by your rules of use to protect them.
- Action speaks louder than words – explain what mixed information is and how to avoid sending it. Discuss why you might misunderstand behaviours such as flirting, texting, or posting pictures online. Help your teen recognize this behaviour and understand how to respond correctly. Make sure they know what incorrect responses are and how to deal with them.
- Daily communication – providing food, clothes, shelter, toys, activities, etc. are all part of being a good parent. However, the most important thing to give them is your time. Talk to your teen every day, and don't stop the rapport when they back off or try to disappoint you. In this way, you can effectively tell your precious teenagers that you are always available and ready to listen to everything they care about. Having regular, open and comfortable conversations can make them feel any worries or fears. Think of the time you spend in discussions every day as an investment in adolescent happiness, which will continue into adulthood.

How Can We Protect Ourselves from Fraud?

Scammers are becoming more or more sophisticated in obtaining money or personal information. Follow our tips to be alert and protect yourself from fraud.

Scam for Everyone

The scams target people of all backgrounds, ages and income levels in Australia. No one is more likely to be a victim of a scam. All of us possibly vulnerable to fraud at some point.

Scams succeed because they look like real things, and you will be caught off guard when you don't expect it. Scammers are getting smarter and using new technologies, new products or services, and significant events to create credible stories that will convince you to tell their money or personal details.

Protect Yourself

Be alert to the fact that there is a scam. When dealing with unwelcome contacts from individuals or businesses, whether by phone, mail, email, in person or on social networking sites, and you should always consider this method as a scam. Remember, if it seems too good to be true, it may be.

- Know who you are dealing with. If you only meet someone online or are unsure of the legitimacy of a business, please take some time to do more research. Do a Google image search on photos, and search the Internet for other people who might be dealing with them. If the message or email is from a friend and it looks abnormal or out of date, please contact your friend directly to check if they sent it.
- Do not open suspicious text, pop-up windows, or click links or attachments in emails – delete them: If you are not sure, please verify the identity of the contact through independent sources such as phone book and online search. Do not use the contact details given in the message sent to you.
- Even if they mention well-known companies such as Telstra, don't respond to calls about your computer requesting remote access-hang up. Scammers will normally ask you to turn on your computer to solve the problem or install a free upgrade. This virus is a virus that can provide you with your password and personal details.
- Keep your details safe. Lock the mailbox, shred bills and other essential documents, and then throw them away. Store your password and PIN in a safe place. Please pay attention to how much personal information you share on social media sites. Scammers can use your information and pictures to create fake identities or target fraud.

- Ensure the safety of your mobile device and computer. Always use password protection, do not share access rights with others (including remote), update security software and back up content. Use a password to protect your Wi-Fi network and avoid using public computers or Wi-Fi hotspots to access online banks or provide personal information.
- Please choose your password carefully. Choose a password that is challenging for others to guess and update regularly. A strong password should contain a combination of uppercase and lowercase letters, numbers and symbols. Do not use the same password for every account/personal profile, and do not share your password with anyone.
- Check your privacy or security settings on social media. If you use social networking sites (such as Facebook), please pay attention to who you contact and understand how to use your privacy and security settings to ensure safety. If you find suspicious behaviour, click spam or have been fraudulent online, please take steps to protect your account and make sure to report it.
- Beware of any requests for detailed information or money from you. Never send money and provide credit card details, online account details or copies of personal files to anyone you don't know or trust. Do not agree to transfer money and goods for others: money laundering is a criminal offence.
- Beware of abnormal payment requests. Scammers will often ask you to use unique payment methods, including pre-installed debit cards, gift cards, iTunes cards, or virtual currencies (such as Bitcoin).
- Be careful when shopping online. Beware of offers that seem incredible, and always use online shopping services that you know and trust. Before using virtual currencies (such as Bitcoin), think twice-they don't have the same protections as other methods of trading, which means you can't get your funds back once you send money. Learn more about online shopping fraud.

How to Find Fakes

Find Clues to Forged Documents

Documents are easy to forget. Some look like real things, but some may have warning signs, such as:

- General rather than a personal greeting
- Organization name that does not exist
- Poor presentation quality
- Inadequate grammar and spelling
- Too official or forced language.

Documents such as flight itineraries or bank statements have a simple, simple layout even when legal because such businesses enable their customers to print online reports. This indicates that scammers can easily create fake documents using information available online, such as company logos and graphics on websites.

Find Clues to Fake Emails

Scammers can easily fake official-looking emails using the same logo and design as the real company.

If you receive an email from a company you've dealt with before (for example, Australia Post or the online shopping site you use), your guards usually crash. If you do not wish to receive emails, please always be alert for fakes before clicking any links or opening any attachments.

Find Clues to Fake Dating Profiles

When viewing new appointment profiles, please note the following unusual choices regarding:

- photo
- position
- hobby
- Language skills match the background.

Scammers often use fake photos found on the Internet.

Tip: Do an image search of admirers to help determine if they are what they say. You can apply image search services such as Google and Tin Eye.

Follow Up Fraud

Scammers will often try to use their strengths when you feel vulnerable and try to get more money from you through subsequent scams.

Some typical follow-up scams include:

- Quotes from law enforcement agencies to investigate your fraud and charge a fee to recover your funds. Law enforcement agencies do not charge service fees.
- Call your doctor to remind you that the scammer needs to pay medical expenses urgently, otherwise, and he may die.
- A lady contacted you to explain that she was the wife of a liar and wanted to escape him, but needed money to do so.

These are just some follow-up methods that scammers might try to get more from you. The new approach may be very different from the original scam and may appear sooner or later. The scammer may have passed your details to other scammers using a completely different method, and the new way does not seem to be related to the original scam.